DOUBLE BOND
an anthology of prairie women's fiction

DOUBLE BOND

an anthology of prairie women's fiction

edited by
Caroline Heath

Fifth House
Saskatoon, Saskatchewan

1984

Canadian Cataloguing in Publication Data
Main entry under title:
Double bond

   ISBN 0-920079-11-3 (bound). — ISBN 0-920079-09-1 (pbk.)

   1. Short stories, Canadian (English) - Prairie Provinces.* 2. Short stories, Canadian (English) - Women authors.* 3. Canadian fiction (English) - Women authors.* 4. Canadian fiction (English) - 20th century. I. Heath, Caroline, 1941 -
PS8329.5.P7D68 1984   C813'.01'089287
PR9197.33.W65D68 1984   C84-091418-0

This book has been published with the assistance of the Saskatchewan Arts Board

Published by
Fifth House
406 Clarence Ave. S.
Saskatoon, Saskatchewan
S7H 2C7

Typeset by
Apex Design Graphics
Saskatoon, Saskatchewan

Printed by
Hignell Printing
Winnipeg, Manitoba

Cover: ''Omen Provided''
by Jane Turnbull Evans

CONTENTS

ACKNOWLEDGEMENTS

'God's Country' by Joan Clark: *From a High Thin Wire,* NeWest Press

'Threshing Time' by Merna Summers: *Calling Home,* Oberon Press

'Das Engelein Kommt' by Gertrude Story: *Sundogs,* Coteau Books; *83: Best Canadian Stories,* Oberon Press

'O What Venerable and Reverend Creatures' by Sharon Butala: *Coming Attractions,* Oberon Press

'The Soma Building' by Beverly Harris: *Three times Five,* NeWest Press

3 poems = 1 story by Gloria Sawai: *Three times Five,* NeWest Press

$$3p = 1\ s$$

$$\frac{p = s}{3}$$

'Snow Flurries' by Brenda Riches: CBC Anthology

'Crush' by Bonnie Burnard: *Coming Attractions,* Oberon Press

'Companionship' by Edna Alford: *A Sleep Full of Dreams,* Oolichan Books

'Various Miracles: A Roundup' by Carol Shields: Canadian Forum

'Falling in Love' by Sandra Birdsell: Arts Manitoba

'The Night Watchman' by Lois Simmie: *Pictures,* Fifth House

Joan Clark

GOD'S COUNTRY

From the beginning Emily felt self-conscious about taking the mine tour. Anybody would feel slightly foolish taking a tour in her old home town, paying money, buying a ticket to view something she'd grown up with. It was a bald admission of ignorance, of not having known enough about Harbour Mines when she'd lived here, of having missed something so important that after another life somewhere else, in Emily's case twenty years, she had to come back to find it.

Though she had disguised herself as a social studies teacher who was here to learn something about the mining industry, Emily knew she was fooling herself. She couldn't help wanting the man in the ticket booth to have the angular face and brown eyes of Damien Roscoe. But the man in front of her pushing a ticket through the makeshift window was short and blue-eyed. She was annoyed at herself for expecting to see Damien. It would be pure coincidence to find him here and anyway what did she think they could possibly say to each other after all these years?

Emily went outside and sat on a bench in the sun. The bench was lobster red and shiny as if it had been painted the day before. She leaned back against the grey shed and closed her eyes, remembering how when she lived here, the daughter of school teacher parents, she had thought of miners as going off to war, knowing that those men who left their houses every morning tunnelled underneath the ocean in a black trench roofed over by sea bottom. A no-man's land. People seldom spoke of it, of the casualties: the cave-ins, the gassings, the accidents. No one would have toured the pit any more than they would have toured a mine field. Back then it wasn't customary for busses of school children to be driven to factories, plants and mines for social studies projects. It was enough to see the miners downtown Saturday night before the nine o'clock show, spending their wages in the British-Canadian Co-op, the People's Store, the OK. It was enough to see them reeling out of the tavern onto the cinder parking lot cursing and brawling. And then in church Sunday mornings, faces scrubbed red and cowlicks plastered down, sitting there subdued, good Christian soldiers.

"Be another ten minutes yet." A dapper man wearing a bow tie and white shirt beneath overalls had come out of the shed and was walking toward Emily.

He stuck out his hand. "Jim Macdonald's the name."

Emily gave him her name. "But I used to be a Prentice," she said.

Mr. Macdonald tipped back his hard hat and scratched his head. "Prentice. Prentice. Don't I know that name from somewheres?"

"My parents were teachers here. I grew up in Harbour Mines."

"So that's it. I knew the name was familiar." Then pretending to scold, Mr. Macdonald said, "What's the matter with you that you're not living here now?"

"I live out West with my family. I teach school there."

"One of those blue-eyed Arabs eh?" He shot her a sly look. "Getting rich off us poor fellas down here."

Emily didn't rise to the bait. Mr. Macdonald knew as well as she did that Cape Breton oil came from Venezuela not Alberta.

"You don't need oil," she said, challenging him. "Look at the coal." She nodded toward the black mounds near the railway tracks, 'the heaps', they were called. "You can burn those."

"Nobody wants our coal," Mr. Macdonald said. "That's why the colliery shut down."

"Well, at least there's enough to keep the furnaces going for a long time," Emily said.

Mr. Macdonald laughed at that. "You've been gone a long time, Lady," he said. "Our coal furnaces were hauled away to the scrap pile years ago and replaced by oil furnaces. A crying shame it was but we can't turn back the clock now can we?"

As if to answer Emily studied the faces of the three miners who sat opposite her. None of them looked familiar. She wasn't sure she'd recognize Damien Roscoe even if she did see him. She had a newspaper photograph of him back home in her photo album but it was fuzzy-grey, out-of-focus; it wasn't any more use than the photograph which hung in an oval frame on her bedroom wall in Calgary. The photograph was of her dead grandmother whom she'd never seen.

The Roscoes had lived in the house next door. They had come from Wales where Mr. Roscoe's father and grandfather had been miners. Mr. Roscoe was tall, black-haired and fierce. His skin was so dark that Emily used to imagine that coal dust had gotten into his pores and into his blood, that his spit was black, even the wax in his ears. She was always surprised when he appeared on his porch or in the parlor window without his shirt, his long underwear unbuttoned to the waist, showing an incongruously pale chest, the hairs looking like black wires stuck into a peeled potato. Sometimes when he was dressed like this, he would sing hymns. He sang tenor standing beside the piano in the parlor while Peggy, the eldest, played. Danny and Damien sang too and Megan, the youngest. Even timid Mrs. Roscoe.

Mr. Roscoe had gotten a choir together, miners who enjoyed singing. They never sang publicly. They never got that far. It was Mr. Roscoe's temper that broke them up. It was nothing for him to jab someone in the chest if he didn't like what was said, to hurtle a plate across the room if the food didn't suit. Both Danny and Damien had been bruised by his belt. Sometimes Mr. Roscoe roared so loud it seemed the shingles of his house shuddered. Emily was always on guard against these dark and sudden outbursts. Even when he was sitting placidly on his front step in his underwear, Emily knew that Mr. Roscoe had only momentarily stepped out of his bearskin, that it was hanging on the hook in the hallway ready to be put back on. Sometimes if she was sitting on the

veranda, he would call out pleasantries to her, about the
freshness of the breeze, the greenness of the grass and
how she was doing in school?

Emily never allowed herself to be drawn past a polite
response. She thought being friendly toward Mr. Roscoe
somehow betrayed Damien's confidence in her. It was
Damien who had told her about the beatings and the
smashed china.

Damien looked like his father's paper cutout. He was
tall and thin with black hair and dark skin but he had
none of his father's robustness. Those times when he was
in bed with bronchitis, Emily brought him his homework. All through junior high school they did their
homework together, coloring maps, writing definitions
out of the same dictionary, copying each other's notes.

Whenever Emily brought home Damien's work, Mrs.
Roscoe ushered her into the parlor. By then Damien was
downstairs waiting for her, sitting on the chesterfield in
his blue-checkered bathrobe. Emily kept her eyes off the
hair that was beginning to show on his legs where his
pajamas rode up. She did not want any reminders that
Damien was becoming a man, that he would one day
need the same things of her as her father had needed.
She avoided looking at the whisker eruptions on his chin,
the tapered strength of his fingers. Instead she concen-
trated on the cleanliness and order of the Roscoe's parlor.
Because it was so different from her mother's careless
housekeeping. Every spring Mrs. Roscoe repapered
walls, painted woodwork, washed doilies and polished
the piano with its shrine of family photos on top. After
Emily had showed Damien his assignments, Mrs. Roscoe
came in with tea and cookies on a tray. The teacups were
Dutch blue with houses on them. Emily never got used

to this. She felt like royalty. As if something more than delivering homework was expected of her. At home her parents served tea in mugs. Visitors had to shove books off chairs in order to sit down. Emily interpreted the good china as meaning Mrs. Roscoe approved of her as Damien's girlfriend. She was uncomfortable with this possibility. In her mind's eye the word *girlfriend* loomed large on a billboard with DANGER and WARNING stickers pasted on top.

Damien was the only Roscoe who was good at school. Peggy had quit grade nine to work as a housekeeper at the hospital. It was too soon to tell about Megan; she was only in grade one. Danny hated school. He wanted to quit, Damien said, but the old man wouldn't let him. He was determined to send Danny to a conservatory for voice lessons, something he had always wanted to do himself. Danny wanted to work in the pit. He went there every chance he got. Damien couldn't figure out why anyone would choose to work in such a dark stinking hole. He'd gone down once with the old man and that was enough. it was so bloody cold he couldn't keep his teeth from chattering. He wanted to get as far away from Harbour Mines as he could. Whenever he talked to Emily about his future, Damien always spoke with fearless bravado, there was nothing he couldn't do. After graduation he was getting a job in the city but only for a year or two until he earned the money for voice lessons. Then he'd get a scholarship to university and work toward a music degree. Someday he'd be a famous singer. He was fifteen when he told Emily this.

"Whatever happened to the Roscoe boys?" Emily said though she already knew about Danny. Mr. Macdonald

and she had been going over different people in town
seeing whom they had both known so it was inevitable
that they should come to the Roscoes.

"Danny's on TV. You must've seen him," Mr. Macdonald said. "Or don't you bother watching us down
here in God's country? Maybe," he gave her a sidelong
look, "Maybe you watch all them Yankee programs."

On Saturday nights Emily liked to go downstairs to
watch Jolly Danny Roscoe on TV. She liked to do this
alone. She never lost the wonder of someone from back
home being on her television screen, a wonder she could
never explain to her husband and kids. Danny was one
of the stars on the Cape Breton Islanders Show; the other
star was hymn singer Gracie Murphy. Danny moved
across the floor in the graceful shuffle Emily had come
to expect of fat people. He'd taken up tap dancing, she'd
supposed, because his voice had run out from hard living and drink. Sometimes he'd take a mouth organ out
of his pocket and puff good-naturedly into it but he could
only play with one hand so it wasn't done with any skill;
it was for comic relief. He seemed so impervious to
ridicule that Emily wondered if off screen he smashed
china and jabbed people.

"He's made a pretty good living for himself, Danny
has," Mr. Macdonald said approvingly. He didn't mention Damien.

They were in grade ten when Damien made a move.
Walking home from school together Damien would suddenly take her hand and hold it in his. She didn't want
to hurt his feelings so she never told him she didn't want
this. Instead she tried to remember to keep both hands
wrapped around her books. She pretended not to notice

where he had written D loves E on his bookcovers.

They had been to a high school dance together, Emily in a blue bengaline dress out of the catalogue, a step up from her mother's dreadful sewing, Damien in Danny's navy blue blazer, the sleeves inches too short for his long arms. Like the other pairs of stick figures, they moved two steps sideways, one back, across the gym floor, the crepe paper streamers pulled into a tent above their heads. She was safe enough here.

The time he picked to kiss her was walking home afterwards along the back streets where the lamp posts were widely spaced and there were tunnels of murky air between them. It was a tender kiss, his lips were soft, insistent. He put his hands on either side of her head, tilting it back. Tilting her gently. Beneath her feet ground shifted dangerously. She ducked down. His hands held her, cupped warm on her shoulders.

"Don't be scared," he said, "I would never hurt you." He bent forward to kiss her again, eyes closed.

This time Emily got away. She ran through the tunnelled air, hair flying, mouth agape.

Behind her she heard him call, "Don't. Don't run."

At the corner where there was light she glanced back and saw Damien two street lights away, hands in his pockets, slouching along, letting her go.

After that she started getting up earlier in the mornings and driving to school with her parents. She waited for them after school so she wouldn't meet Damien. If there was homework she sent it over with Megan.

Peggy Roscoe passed her by on the street without speaking. Though she'd quit school, Peggy still had a girlfriend in grade twelve so the news was out — Emily was stuck up. She thought she was too good for Damien.

This was partly true. Emily thought Damien should have been made of sterner stuff, that he shouldn't have given up so easily. When he got a steady girlfriend a few months later, she disowned ever having known him. She left Harbour Mines when she was seventeen, determined to disown it too.

For a long time after she'd moved away, she went so far as to lie about having lived in Harbour Mines. If someone asked her about where she'd grown up, she'd say Cape Breton. If pressed she'd say in a vague sort of way, oh a small place near Sydney, you wouldn't know it. She felt ashamed of this now.

Harbour Mines hadn't changed much since she'd left; it was still the same size. But her perception of the landscape had changed. It wasn't monochromatic grey as she had remembered it but blatantly technicolor. It seemed every color on the paint charts had been used. The town hall was teal blue, the school forest green, the churches robin's egg blue, moss green, maroon. Down here near the mine the houses looked like brightly painted codfish boxes strung along lengths of rope tossed overboard into a sea of green scrub. Some of the streets had houses on one side only. Here and there front steps hadn't been built deliberately cutting off access to the parlour, preserving the sanctity of carpeting and color TV. Yards were treeless: trees here did not do well. There was no protection against the winter wind that swept off the ice floes in Cabot Strait.

Emily wondered if Damien lived down here somewhere. She knew he'd sold the big house next door. Her mother had mentioned that years ago in a letter. When Emily had written back asking where did he go, her

mother's reply was that she'd no idea, he might have
moved off the island altogether for all she knew.

Emily doubted that. He'd left leaving too late. Probably he'd become one of those Cape Bretoners who
couldn't leave, who believed this island, this rock of red
cliffs and green hills was God's country. Maybe it was
to catch God's eye that they used so much bright paint.

As she sat on the bench Emily imagined what it would
be like bumping into Damien. Coincidentally, of course.
She'd ask him about his family. He'd married early, her
mother had said, there were four kids close together.
Maybe she'd go home with him. Have tea. She might
even talk him into singing something for her. She'd keep
the conversation light. There would be no mention of
the past. She couldn't tell him now — any more than
she could then — that her running away had to do not
with him but with her father. He wouldn't remember
anyway. Her wanting to see Damien had to do with
knowing she'd disowned him, of living that down. She
wanted to do this even though she knew that this was
an indulgence that more than anything else made her
a tourist in Harbour Mines.

"What's Damien doing now?" She finally came out
and asked because Mr. Macdonald hadn't said a word
about him. She was beginning to think he was deliberately avoiding the subject but when he answered she thought
she understood why.

"He's retired," Mr. Macdonald said, 'Same as the
rest of us.''

Emily knew retired meant laid off, *unemployed.* Had
Damien become another hospitalized war veteran spending winter in thermostatically controlled rooms, summer warming himself on a sunny bench at the minehead

watching tourists like herself? Or had he found other things to do, organized a choir perhaps?

"You just might see him around," Mr. Macdonald said. "He comes down here sometimes if the weather's nice. If I see him, I'll tell him you were asking for him."

Another miner came up. He was rotund and ruddy-cheeked and, she guessed, bald beneath his hard hat. He reminded her of Danny Roscoe.

"The tour's starting," he said to her. "You'd better come with me."

"Isn't that just like an O'Hara," Mr. Macdonald said, "trying to horn in."

"She's done with you," O'Hara grinned. "It's me she wants now."

"Now there's an Irishman for you," Mr. Macdonald said, "Always thinks the women are after him."

"Listen to that would you!" O'Hara turned to Emily. "These Scotchmen think they own the whole island. Talk about hogs."

Mr. Macdonald adjusted his bow tie.

"If he gives you any trouble, you just report him to me."

Inside there was more of the same. Emily presented her ticket but O'Hara waved it away. She jammed the ticket into her jeans pocket, hooked her jacket onto one of the gaffs hanging from the shed beams and went into the room where they stored the gear. There another miner, much younger than O'Hara, with buck teeth, was handing out flashlights. When he went to strap on Emily's, O'Hara took the flashlight from him and fastened the belt around her waist so that the battery hung just above her hip. Then he looped the cord over her shoulder so she could manoeuver the flashlight in front. He fiddled with the cord making sure it was the right length. The other miner stood there; bucktooth grinning, leaning one elbow against the shelf.

"What a way with women you have, O'Hara," he said.

"Jealousy will get you nowheres."

"I'm not jealous. I'm full of admiration. I'm just standing here hoping to pick up a few pointers."

O'Hara put a red poncho over Emily's shoulders.

"It'll keep you clean."

And a hard hat.

"Regulations. You wouldn't want to hit your head on a tie."

"Hey O'Hara, don't take all night," one of the miners yelled. "We got seven others ready to go down."

Beside the two men, students they looked like, there was a family of five, three school-aged daughters and their parents, campers, probably on their way to the Cabot Trail. O'Hara picked up a pointer and indicated the elevator. They got on. The door clanked shut. They started down. The elevator was an open cage with grey metal bars badly rusted. Water dripped off the sides of the shaft. Emily heard it splashing below.

The elevator cage thudded to the bottom. The door grated open. It was black, cold and wet.

"Put your flashlights on and follow me. Watch the water," O'Hara said; he was all business now.

Flashlights on, they followed O'Hara past puddled water. At the entrance to a tunnel, O'Hara stopped.

"This mine goes six miles under the sea, 2360 feet down to be exact, but we're only going to 680. We'll be following the rail line. Keep your heads down and watch your step. She drops a foot every ten feet so we'll be walking on a slant."

12

There were dim lights strung out at intervals along the tunnel and as they bent over, crab-walking the ties, Emily was able to see that the mine walls were shored up with heavy timbers and iron ties irregularly spaced. The whole mass had been sprayed with white powder to retard fire. The yellow lights and white powder gave a sulphurous thickness to the air.

They came out of the tunnel to a higher ceilinged cave that was an intersection where the main tunnel plunged down and a smaller tunnel went off to a coal seam. O'Hara took them into the room where the engine controlled the cable drum, the cable that ran the coal cars to the tunnel bottom and back up. There were WARNING and DANGER signs pasted on the walls, large numbered instructions.

"This is the most important piece of equipment in the mine," O'Hara said "Used to be up on top. But after the accident she was moved down here."

"What accident?" one of the daughters wanted to know.

"Cable broke. Fourteen men were killed."

Mr. Roscoe was in one of the cars that was cut off, racing out of control, plummeting down the tunnel, gathering speed, down, down the sulphurous walls flashing past, stomachs sucked out, chests ripped open, eyes squeezed shut on inner darkness, the last chilling minutes careening past.

Despite Mr. Roscoe's temper, the Anglican church couldn't hold all the miners who came to the funeral. Emily went with her parents. She remembered her father saying the music would have made the old boy proud. Although Danny had come home for the funeral, it was Damien who sang the twenty-fourth psalm. He was eighteen then and his voice had come out of the change a tenor.

Outside the engine room, Emily caught sight of a grey stag's head. It was lumpily constructed and clumsily painted with red spots for eyes and antlers too thick for realism but there was no mistaking it was a stag's head.

O'Hara saw her looking at it.

"Some of the men made that. Used grease from the machine. Sort of built it up with blobs that fell off. The leftovers like. Did a good job, I'd say."

Emily stared at the eyes hoping she would see pupil dots emerge and dilate so she could see inside the stag's head, to know there were pictures inside it: meadows open and green, maple groves, autumn sunshine, colored leaves. But the eyes remained blank, painted shut with what looked like nail polish.

O'Hara was leading them into another tunnel. Hunched over, their hats bumping rock, they switched on their flashlights and followed. This tunnel didn't open up even when they reached the coal face, so they had to stay bent over while O'Hara explained things. Emily put her handbag down and sat on that.

"You couldn't have done that when the mine was operating or the rats would've crawled right up your pantlegs," O'Hara said.

Below her jeans the meat of Emily's tanned ankle was exposed as tender white against the black coal. She got up quickly.

O'Hara laughed. "Don't worry. When the men left, the rats left. But boys o'boys when they were here, you had to look out. We tied string around our cuffs so they wouldn't crawl up our legs. When you opened up your lunch pail, you had to kick 'em off with your boot. I

14

always went back to where the tunnel opens up so I could eat standing up.'' Here the light bulbs were larger and closer together so visibility was better. But the shadows were blacker. The light shone on the layered coal face glittering like rats' eyes.

''This machine is what gets the coal out of the seam. See, it's got a jack to hold up the roof while it digs out the coal. It goes in so far then moves sideways. We always used this. Never used a pick and shovel.''

The machine had a huge rounded saw-toothed blade that rotated when O'Hara switched it on. The blade moved forward, chewing into the seam. Chunks of coal dropped easily, tumbling into a cart. A black cloud of coal dust puffed out. The noise, rolled into a hard probing core, drilled into Emily's ears.

O'Hara switched off the machine and directed their attention to the coal cars.

''With the machine doing the digging, we had a devil of a job keeping up with it. The empty cars kept moving in. We had to keep moving the full ones out. Had to be quick about it or you'd jam your hand.''

That was what happened to Danny Roscoe. After the old man was killed there was nothing to keep him out of the mine. But he'd only worked down here a few months when he jammed his right hand between two cars. Broke the bones. Pulped them to sausage meat. It didn't show on the television screen. Danny had become skilful at keeping it behind his back or tucked inside his jacket front against his chest as if he really was singing those true-blue love songs from his heart.

Damien quit grade twelve after that to work in the mine. There was no other money coming in. Peggy had married a farmer and moved to Margaree. It was a year

before Danny's hand healed and he was able to get a
job with a pick-up band playing Saturday night dances.
Even then he wasn't paid much and there was Megan
to get through school.

"You want some coal for souvenirs, this is your
chance," O'Hara said. He took out plastic bags and
handed them round.

Emily couldn't imagine a piece of coal as a souvenir.
What was it a souvenir of anyway? Would they be handing out jars of tar sand and oil someday? She was surprised at O'Hara. She would have thought that handing
out coal as a momento somehow cheapened the risk in
getting it.

But O'Hara didn't seem to mind. He was helping the
little girls load up their bags.

Emily's back ached from bending over. How did the
men stand it, hunched over all day in the cold and damp?
She straightened up and her plastic hard hat hit metal.
She looked up and saw it had hit a horseshoe nailed to
a beam.

After Emily had moved out West, her mother used
to send her the Harbour Mines newspaper tied up in
brown paper and string third class mail. Sometimes it
was months before she looked through the pile of weeklies
and then it was only a quick glance before throwing them
out. But she read every word of the cave-in. Clipped out
from the front page and folded it into her photo album.
Eight men were trapped. Six days of no food, water, fresh
air, the coal wedged tight around them. One of the men,
it had to be an Irishman, was quoted as saying he knew
they'd be rescued because there was a horseshoe nailed

to a beam, they could feel it in the dark. Another miner, an Englishman, said it was Damien singing to them that kept their spirits up. Down there in the dark, he said, Damien sounded like a nightingale. There was a photograph of Damien on the front page. He looked old, haggard, his eyes staring whitely from blackened skin. He looked like someone returned from the dead.

There was a last stop in the mine tour, at the tipple that dumped the coal cars onto the conveyor belt that took the coal out, before O'Hara had them riding the cars up the long slope to the surface, the fresh air rushing down to meet them. At the top they took off their gear and returned it to the shed.

Emily stepped outside to blinding July sunlight, to the plaintive wail of bagpipes. A girl in kilt and lace was playing "Road to the Isles." Behind her unrolled a tartan of green swamp and blue sea, the water woven through with yellow threads.

Mr. Macdonald was waiting for her. Beside him was a tall man, badly stooped, with a polka dot ascot at his neck. Damien. Just when she was beginning to wonder if she should ask Mr. Macdonald where he lived. He looked old, a paler version of the miner in the photograph. Without the coal dust and with his hair turned white he no longer looked like his father's paper cutout, but the silhouette surrounding it.

"This is the fellow you were asking about," Mr. Macdonald said unnecessarily.

Emily took a step forward and stuck out a nervous hand.

"Do you remember me? I used to live next door to you."

He looked so aged Emily thought he might have forgotten her.

But he didn't. He took her hand, squeezing the fingers hard.

"How are you, Damien?" she said.

Damien smiled. He wore dentures, she noticed, and had shrinkage lines on his upper lip. The lips, thin now, pulled back and a faint F came out. A voiceless F. An F squeezed out and shaped by a wheeze of air.

"He says he's fine," Mr. Macdonald interpreted.

But Emily didn't get it right away. It didn't register fast enough. Both men must have seen the disbelief on her face.

Mr. Macdonald helped her out. "Damien had an operation two years ago. Had his voice box removed. A plastic one put in. He's doing pretty good with it, wouldn't you say?"

Emily stood there holding Damien's hand unable to let go of it, unable to speak.

So Mr. Macdonald went on. "These Welshmen are terrible fellas. Stubborn as mules. You wouldn't believe how stubborn they are. You can't get rid of one no matter how hard you try."

But even with Mr. Macdonald's help, Emily couldn't say what she wanted to say. What she wanted to say, now that he was finally in front of her, was: *I loved you, Damien. Once a long time ago I really loved you.* But there was a risk in saying this even to herself. The risk was not that Damien would be indifferent to this admission or think her guilty of foolish exaggeration but that it might be mistaken for pity.

"He may have trouble speaking," Mr. Macdonald was prodding her, "but he has no trouble listening."

Slowly, with her other hand, Emily took the crumpled

ticket out her jeans pocket and held it up for Damien to see.

"Look," she said, staring at it, "I bought a ticket. I must say it seemed strange buying a ticket. I mean to go down and see the place where you and your father and brother worked. They sell tickets to all sorts of things nowadays, don't they?" She was babbling, she knew, trying too hard. "Would you believe just last week in Calgary, I bought a ticket . . ." she looked up then to engage Mr. Macdonald but he had walked quietly away. She wanted to run after him. She felt a tightening around her hand. There was a wheezing sound.

Emily looked at Damien's mouth. She saw his tongue curl upward. She felt the soft explosion of air against her cheek. She watched the lips funnelling a *D*. The *D*, disembodied — separate from Damien — floated past her ear.

"Don't run," he was saying.

The 'away' was indiscernible, gulped down with an intake of air. But the next words were distinct enough; a *T* exploded.

"This time," he said and grinned. Then with a gentlemanly grace which Emily remembered he always had even in his own parlor, he indicated a bench they could sit on.

They talked about their families, people they had both known, the energy crisis, the weather. Though Damien kept smiling and nodding, wheezing unselfconsciously and the summer sun warmed the lobster red bench where they sat, Emily could not tear her mind from the dark tunnels below. She wanted to go back down the mine, to pry out the nails, bring the horseshoe up here, to hurtle it skyward, but it was such a pitiful, useless tool for smashing the eye of God.

Merna Summers

THRESHING TIME

There were three people in the room, counting the child. The house they were sitting in belonged to the smaller man, but a stranger coming into the room might have thought otherwise. The small man, whose name was Black, was seated in a rocking-chair, but he was not rocking. Instead, he was leaning forward, so far forward that only the front arc of his rockers made contact with the floor. He looked as if he might be waiting for some sign — to speak, perhaps, or to jump to his feet to perform some task.

It was the big man, the older man, who was at his ease. His name was Max Staunton. He sat on the Winnipeg couch, leaning back, his eyes surveying the room. There was not very much in it to look at, but what there was his eyes took in. They took in the printed curtain hanging across the doorway to the front bedroom. They took in the sewing-machine treated as a table, with a cloth on top. They took in the unlighted lamp and its clean chimney. When they came to the corner of the room, they took in the radio. It was a small one and it sat on a cloth-skirted box. Its striped batteries were on the floor beneath, but the wires that should have connected radio and batteries to outdoor aerial had been yanked from the wall; they curled crazily in the air.

Staunton's eyes stopped and considered the wires. Finally, "Radio not working?" he asked.

Black looked embarrassed.

"It works if it's connected," he said.

The third person in the room, the child, was seated on Staunton's lap, but her body wasn't adjusted for lap-sitting. She held herself stiffly, as carefully as if she were perched on a high rail fence. Staunton was a stranger to father and daughter alike, but the daughter was at an additional disadvantage: she could not see the man. All she knew of him was what she could tell by feel. That and what she had seen when he arrived a few minutes before.

Black had been sitting on the back porch mending harness when Staunton's car drove into the yard. The child was beside him. They looked up and where a moment before there had been only pin-cherry bushes and the dooryard gate, there now was a man. He was big: tall and powerfully built, but big-bellied with middle age.

Staunton saw them at the same time as they saw him, and when he saw them, he stopped. He hooked his thumbs through the belt of his trousers and smiled. He had an unusual way of smiling. His bottom lip came out when he did it.

"I'm looking for a fellow by the name of Owen Black," he said.

Owen stood up. "You just found him," he said.

They shook hands then, and went into the house, the child following them. Staunton was at his ease from the very first, his eyes looking around freely. He might have been trying to assure Owen that he had been coming into such places all his life.

Staunton had lifted the child onto his lap when he sat down and she remained where he had put her, waiting to find out what was expected of her.

"This is a fine little girl you've got here," Staunton said. His voice was a gentle boom. It was a voice that was at a variance with his appearance, but Owen didn't notice that. He didn't meet many strangers; he didn't get much practice in assessing them.

"Your daddy's a lucky man to have a nice little girl like you," Staunton said to the child, whose name was Estelle.

"I don't have any little people at my house." He tilted his head back and his bottom lip came out as he smiled. "My little boy got to be big a long time ago," he said.

Something about the way he spoke suggested that Max Staunton was performing for an invisible audience. It was as if there was another Max Staunton standing by watching, a man whose approval he counted on.

The child did not move. There was an awareness of strangeness in her face. There was strange flesh — strange thing, strange arm — brought into contact, almost into contact, with her own flesh. She hadn't been able to decide how to feel about it.

She was wearing a thin cotton dress with a sash at the waist. Her arms and legs were bare. She wore canvas shoes, darned at the toes, but no stockings. Her feet and legs protruded awkwardly, in the position they had taken when Staunton put her where she was. She made no attempt to move. It was as if to her mind, to slide away, to reclaim possession of her own body, was an act somehow related to disobedience. A thought not thinkable.

At ordinary times Owen took pride in his daughter's silence, her compliance with visitors, but at the moment he wasn't thinking about her at all. He was thinking about Staunton. He had heard of Staunton before, but this was the first time he had seen him. It seemed to Owen that the man was different from what he would have expected.

In what way, different? Owen couldn't say. Confronted with the reality, Owen couldn't remember what it was that he had been expecting. Or say how Staunton differed from it. Owen's thoughts didn't come to him in words.

From the kitchen there came the sound of a stove lid being lifted and replaced, and then the clink of water dipper against tea kettle. If Owen had been asked what the sounds meant, he could have told you that Josie was in the kitchen making coffee. But he wasn't asked, and his mind didn't comment.

"I suppose you've heard that I'm in the market for men," Staunton said then.

Owen nodded. He had heard that. He supposed that was why Staunton was here: to give him a job.

"Not that I expect to have any trouble making up a crew," Staunton said. "There are men growing on the trees this fall." Staunton's hand was toying with a curl of cotton stuffing that had pushed its way through the

24

worn covering of the Winnipeg couch. "Most of the outfits are filled up," he said. "But I can still take on one
more team."

Owen leaned back then, waiting, and the middle of
his rockers made contact with the floorboards. But instead of offering Owen the job, Staunton began to talk
about who he would be threshing. "We start at the
Allsopps' tomorrow," he said. "And then we'll do the
Larsons. And after that, the Beckers."

He had taken out tobacco and papers and was rolling
a cigarette, his arm still around the child. He stopped
speaking to lick the paper. "You'll come after the
Beckers," he told Owen. "That is, *if* I'm doing you."

Owen leaned forward again. He didn't understand
what Staunton was telling him. Of course Staunton
would be threshing him . . . unless he wasn't working for
Staunton. Was Staunton trying to tell him that he might
not get the job?

Owen wished that he knew more about Max Staunton.
He knew that Staunton had bought the Hubble place
south of town last fall, and that he had moved up after
the crops were off. Staunton had come from farther south
in the province. Owen knew that Staunton had a thresh-
ing-machine and that he had a grown son, a boy with
an unusual name. The reason Staunton was threshing
north of town instead of in his own district was that the
north country was short of threshing outfits and the south
wasn't. Owen knew that much about him.

Now it seemed that Staunton wanted to add to his
knowledge. "I've taken off a lot of crops in my day,"
Staunton was saying. He hooked his thumbs through
his belt and smiled. "If I don't know what I'm doing
by now, I guess I never will," he said.

He stopped then, as if he expected that Owen would want to say something. He was smiling, he seemed friendly. But when Owen remained silent, a look that resembled displeasure came on to his face. It was only there for a moment. Then Staunton sort of took it off and put it away, as if in storage.

After a minute, ''Anyway, it's Elreno who runs the outfit now,'' Staunton said pleasantly. ''His old dad is just the flunky.''

Elreno was the name of Staunton's son. Owen had heard that Elreno was his father's tractor man. Staunton himself looked after the separator. But as to who was boss . . . well, Owen had taken it for granted that Staunton would be.

''Elreno's a good man,'' Staunton was saying. He smiled again. ''You know how it will take some men half the night to line up an outfit?'' he said. ''Well, Elreno gets it right first try, every time. And he's never had a belt slide off yet.''

Owen tried to think of something to say. The room they were sitting in was warm. Josie had washed the wooden floor earlier to cool the house off, but the heat was starting to come back.

''I don't say this because he's my son,'' Staunton went on, ''But I can tell you that Elreno is going to be a good man at handling men too.'' He shifted the child from right knee to left. ''That was something I taught him myself,'' he said. And then, as if to explain, ''There are some men that would walk all over you if you didn't stand up for your rights,'' Staunton said.

When he had said that, he stopped again. Again it was as if he thought that Owen would want to say something, but again Owen was silent. And again the look of displeasure crossed Staunton's face.

Owen didn't see it. He was watching Staunton and listening to him, but he wasn't taking in what Staunton was telling him with either his voice or his face. *Offer me a job,* he was thinking. *Offer me a job.*

He had to have a job. Otherwise . . .

There was no otherwise. It had come to this: Estelle had no shoes but the canvas ones she had on her feet, and they had darns in the toes. It had come to this: he and Josie had only one set of winter chore clothes between them; if they had a two-man job to do, they had to wait for a warm day to do it. Josie was making her slips and underdrawers out of flour sacks. Owen couldn't bear to think about them; he turned over in bed and faced the wall every night when she undressed. It had come to this: they owed money for seed and twine and groceries. They did without whatever they could. Some things, like a radio licence, they never even considered buying. Josie had to scramble like a thief to disconnect the radio whenever a strange car slowed down on the road. But there were things they couldn't do without: flour, coal oil, felt socks.

Relief? It was out of the question. Josie's father didn't believe in it. "Any man who can't feed his own family is a pretty poor excuse for a man," he said, and Owen agreed with him. As far as he knew, so did Josie.

But it wasn't easy, staying off relief. There were times when Owen thought that he had reached the breaking point. But he had always hung on somehow. He had felt as if he was going to break down so many times that he no longer took the feeling seriously. He knew that some people really did have breakdowns, but he also knew that he wasn't one of them. He hung on. Only he got so tired.

Owen could remember what it had felt like to enjoy his body, to rejoice in its energies. But now, coming in from the field or from choring, ''I'm no good for anything anymore,'' he would think. Only it wasn't just working that made him tired. He could be tired even after a rainy day. He was so tired all the time that he never really felt like doing anything. He was too tired even for Josie.

Sometimes Josie would be helping him with a job, or he would be helping her. They could be doing anything: digging potatoes, mending binder canvas, banking up the house for winter . . . and it would come into Owen's head that Josie was thinking about *that*. Then he would have to look away. Because there was nothing he could do to help it.

Once, when he would be doing other things, going about his work, he used to find himself thinking about Josie, and what they did together, and the thinking gave him pleasure. He hadn't known then that it would come to an end so soon, before either of them was 30. Nobody had told him that that happened. Somebody should have, he thought. If they had, he would have made hay while the sun shone, so to speak. He wouldn't have wasted a single opportunity.

Now, since there was nothing to be done about it, he preferred not to think about it at all. He put it out of his mind. If he wanted something nice to think about, he thought about Estelle.

It seemed to Owen that the feelings he had about Estelle were not dependent upon her being his daughter. He believed that even if she had belonged to somebody else, he still would have been able to perceive her essential quality, which was purity. He didn't use that word

to describe her, and it was only part of what he meant
when he said, "She's just pure Estelle." The other part
was that there was nothing "put on" about Estelle. She
was the same thing from pith to peel. Compared to her,
other children seemed to Owen to be artificial and
calculating. It seemed to him that they treated themselves
not as people but as things: things that they used to produce effects, to gain attention. Owen was glad that Estelle
wasn't like that.

Sitting on Staunton's lap now, Estelle was less stiff
than she had been, but her eyes were still questioning,
unsure. Staunton seemed to be trying to get her to relax.
He had her hand in his, and her arm on his, and he was
bouncing their two arms up and down together. There
was a cadence to the motion, as when a man dandles
a baby on his foot, or taps his toe to music. But he was
fondling Estelle without really giving her his attention.
His attention was on Owen.

"You know," Staunton said, "there are men around
this fall who want a job so bad they'd crawl to get it."
He shook his head, as if inviting Owen to share his
wonder at how bad things had got to be. Then, "They
told me you were wanting a job," he said.

Owen eased back on his rockers. "They told you
right," he said.

Staunton nodded. "There have been a lot of men after
me for jobs," he said.

Owen felt the need to speak up on his own behalf.
"Those would be men without teams," he said. He
wanted to see things settled. He wanted to remind Staunton that he had a team.

But Staunton looked displeased. "Men with teams and
men without," he said shortly.

Staunton had given up bouncing the child's arm. Now the fingers of his right hand were pulling a piece of stuffing out of the couch. His left hand was cupped over Estelle's knee, and one finger was moving back and forth, back and forth, tracing an arc on the soft skin on the inside of her knee. Both hands busy, but his eyes someplace else. His eyes were on Owen's face.

Estelle's eyes, too, sought her father's.

"It makes it hard for me," Staunton said. "I can't say yes to one without saying no to another."

Owen looked out the window. His eyes came to rest on the pin-cherry bushes. What was it that Staunton wanted him to say? *Whatever deal you're offering, it's all right with me?* That would be the truth, but it wasn't a thing that Owen cared to hear said in words.

"You'd be surprised at how desperate some people are getting," Staunton said.

Josie came in then with the coffee things, and when she had brought them everything they needed, left them alone again.

Then Staunton began to play a tickling game with the child.

"The little wood tick went *here*," he said, and his fingers walked in tiny, tiny footsteps up from her wrist . . . "and *here* . . ." they reached the inside of her elbow. "And *here*!" They invaded the hollow place underneath her arm.

The child collapsed in Staunton's arms, wriggling with pleasure.

Owen shuddered. He wanted to say *You cut that out.* He played tickling games with Estelle himself, but it seemed to him that Staunton's game was different from his game. In his game it was *the little mousie* who crawled up arms. There might have been another difference too, but Owen couldn't put a name to what it was. In any case, the difference between wood ticks and mousies was enough.

As far as he knew, Owen had never seen a wood tick, but as a boy he had been told about them. He had been told that a wood tick could bite you and you wouldn't even feel it. But if you didn't see the wood tick on your skin and get him off by lighting a match and holding it to him, he would eat his way inside of you. And if he got inside, it would be too late. He would eat his way up your bloodstream and when he got to your heart you would die.

Owen was disgusted with himself when he realized that he, a grown man, had been about to speak out over a thing that was silly: the kind of thing that boys invent to scare each other with. Owen didn't even know if such a creature as a wood tick really existed. Even so, he wished that Staunton would stop playing with Estelle. Owen wanted to talk business. Staunton had obviously come to offer him a job. He hadn't come here for any other purpose. What, then, was holding him back?

As soon as Owen put the question to himself, an answer occurred. It could be because of his size.

Owen Black was small man, as he had been a small boy. As a boy, he had learned that survival depended on staying out of fights. As a man, he was learning that it depended on doing more than you had it in you to do. Keeping on: that was what counted. And Staunton might not know it, but Owen could do that. Tired or not, he could keep on going. He had never stopped yet.

Last year had been a killer, but it hadn't killed him. Neither had the year before. He had thought it was going to. In the beginning there was only the dust and the chaff and the itching under your underwear. Later there was the exhaustion. And then the working beyond exhaustion. Sometimes, at the very last, the exhaustion would leave him. At those times Owen seemed to himself to leave his body, to be standing outside of it, not feeling anything. It was as if he were hovering in the air above and looking down at his own body. It seemed very small and far away. But it was still doing its work, still obeying orders.

There was nothing that Staunton could dish out that he couldn't take. Owen wanted to tell him that. He leaned forward, willing Staunton to offer him a job. He wanted to hear it put into words, to know that things were settled.

You want to work for me? Yes, I do. No more than that was needed. There was no need to talk about pay. Staunton would pay what all the outfits were paying this year: $1.50 a day for a man; $2.50 for a man with a team.

Staunton stopped playing with Estelle. Suddenly, "Do you break your own horses?" he asked.

Owen shook his head. He was considered a good man with horses, but he couldn't break them.

"I used to break horses," Staunton said. "When I was younger, I used to be able to swing a line and raise a blister under a horse's coat. I had enough strength in my shoulders for that." he smiled, remembering. "We used to practise," he said. "Some of us young fellows. We'd set up some bottles and then we'd swing our lines at them till we broke them."

He spoke as a man discussing his craft. "If you want to break horses for threshing, you've got to be able to lace them within an inch of their lives," he said. "The only way you can get an unbroke team to go up to the machinery is to make them scareder of what's behind them than what's in front of them.''

Owen nodded. He knew that what Staunton said was true, but he couldn't do it himself. He had got Frank Deacon to break his horses for threshing.

''I'm not too happy about the team I'm putting into the field this year,'' Staunton went on. ''They've threshed before. But I wouldn't say they were broke. A team's not broke until you can trust them.''

Owen was impatient. It was jobs, not horse-breaking, that he wanted to hear talked about. But then Staunton began to do that. Sort of. At least he edged into the topic sideways. He told Owen that he docked his men for moving time. He considered himself a pretty good man to work for, he said, but he had never been able to see why a man should expect to be paid for time when he wasn't doing a blessed thing.

Owen kept his silence. If you didn't agree with a man, there wasn't much you could say to him. He could have told Staunton that people around here didn't think much of a man who docked his men 20¢ every time he moved the separator from one field to another. He felt as if he ought to tell him that, for his own good.

But before Owen could make up his mind to speak, Staunton had begun to talk about working hours. ''Most of the outfits around here are in the field from 6 to 7,'' he said. ''Well, so am I. But I'm not going to shut down at 7 if another hour will get a field finished.''

Suddenly Staunton smiled. He looked like a man who has just thought of a good story.

''A kind of funny thing happened on my outfit last year,'' he said. ''There was a guy working for me by the name of Jake Inkom. The men called him Inky. And Inky was a good worker, I'll say that for him. But he was a born troublemaker. Well, I could see that he was getting to be too big for his britches, that I was going to have to take him down a peg or two. But before I could get around to doing anything about it, he came up to me one day.

"I remember the way he looked when he came up," Staunton said. "There was a wind blowing over the summerfallow across the road from the place where we were picking up, and he was black as a nigger. He looked kind of like a nigger anyway. At least to me he did. And he stood there, with his ears full of the neighbour's summerfallow, and he wanted to know what time I was figuring on quitting that night. The men were getting fed up with working late every night, he said.

" 'Oh,' I said. 'This is the first I've heard of it. Nobody's mentioned it to me.'

'Well they are,' he said.

'Oh, I don't like to hear that,' I said. 'I don't like having men on my outfit who aren't happy.' "

To Owen, "I just let him think that over for a minute," Staunton said. "And then I said, 'I'll tell you another thing I don't like, Inky,' I said. 'I don't like a man who thinks he knows more than I do about how I ought to run my outfit.' I said it loud, so that the other men could hear it. 'If there's any men here who don't like the time I start and the time I stop, I'd appreciate it if they'd say so right now,' I said. 'Because I can find someone to take their place without any trouble at all. And I wouldn't want anybody who wasn't happy working for me.'

"Inky dropped his head then, and I could see his

jawbones grinding. But Inky wasn't a fool. After a minute he went back about his business.

"And you know," Staunton finished, smiling, "I never had no more trouble with him after that."

Owen tried to push his mind around the story Staunton had told him, but it wouldn't go there. He felt tired, as if there was some force pulling at him from inside, drawing him together and making him smaller.

"I think I'm a pretty easy man to get along with," Staunton said. He smiled then, that odd smile with the bottom lip pushed out. "Mind you," he said, "if a man's looking for trouble, I don't mind seeing to it that he gets it."

There was nothing for Owen to say. Nothing in his experience had prepared him to deal with a man like Staunton.

Staunton fixed Owen with his eyes. "I like a man to know what he's getting into when I hire him," he said. "That way, I don't have to listen to any bellyaching later."

Owen looked away. His eyes came to rest on the disconnected wires of the radio, curling crazily in the air. He felt that he had to speak. "I've never had any trouble on any of the outfits I've worked for," he said.

But then he found that he didn't like the sound of what he had said.

"Mind you, I guess I can bellyache as good as the next one," he added.

A hard look came into Staunton's eyes. He turned his attention away from Owen, toward the child. The palm of his hand was on her chest, curved over the place where one day she would have breasts. There were two pockets on the bodice of her dress, one over each breast.

With the forefinger of his right hand, Staunton began
to trace the outline made by rickrack braid around the
right pocket.

The child's face took on a secretive look. It was as
if she knew something, but for reasons of her own was
pretending not to. She sat very still, one end of her sash
between her fingers.

Again Owen felt his lack of experience with strangers.
He could see that Estelle had lost her fear of Staunton.
Her lips were parted and her eyes were half-closed. It
was as if her attention was turned inward.

Staunton shifted Estelle's body from his right knee to
his left, and then his left forefinger began to circle, following the outline of her pocket. The little nipples were visible, stiff as shoe buttons, through the cotton of her dress.

"*Estelle!*"

Owen's voice came out sharp. He startled himself and
the child.

He made himself speak in a more normal voice. "You
run along now," he said. "You've been pestering Mr.
Staunton long enough."

But Staunton's hand stayed on Estelle's chest, holding
her. "She's no bother," he said. "Let her stay where
she is."

It seemed to Owen that there was nothing he could
say. All grownups played with children. If there was
something different about the way Staunton did it, Owen
didn't have a name for what the difference was. Maybe
there was no difference. Maybe it was all in his head.

Staunton's finger had gone back to its gentle circling,
but his attention wasn't on the child now. It was as if
she — as if *Estelle* — did not exist for him. There was
something on his lap and he was fondling it. But the eyes

were on Owen. It was Owen he was getting his pleasure from.

Again Owen felt that force inside of him, pulling him into a smaller knot. What was a man supposed to do? But when he asked himself that question, his thoughts turned aside, retreated. He lowered his eyes before Staunton's steady gaze. They came to rest on Estelle's feet: her canvas shoes, the darned toes of them. He did not speak.

After a moment it seemed to him that Staunton had known he would not speak. Owen stirred then and his rocking-chair creaked. The room had got hotter. He was sweating. He felt as if his body was telling him something. He became aware of hands clutched on the arms of his chair, of toes arched, pressed so hard against the soles of his boots that they ached. His neck felt weak, unable to hold up his head. And then his stomach cramped sharply and he realized that if he didn't get up and walk away from here, he was going to be sick.

He stood up. "I better get back to my harness," he said.

Staunton stood up too. "Not so fast," he said.

He spoke like a man who liked to do the leaving; a man who wouldn't be left. "You haven't told me yet whether you want to work for me or not."

Owen knew what he ought to say. He ought to say *I can stand it if you can.* Something that, by making a joke of it, would make it sound like he had a choice. But he didn't risk it.

"I do," he said.

"All right then," Staunton said. "Be at the Allsopps' for breakfast tomorrow morning."

Then he turned to go. He was the first one out of the house.

On the path, Estelle caught up with Staunton and reached up to take his hand. And then, when Staunton looked down, the child simpered up at him. *She's making eyes,* Owen thought.

Owen followed Staunton and Estelle out to the gate, keeping his eyes fastened on the pin-cherry bushes. Their leaves were red. He did not look at the child, who was prancing, her body motions jerky, showing off.

Owen had no name for the way he was feeling but he did know that there was something that he should have done, and that he hadn't done it. But when should he have done it? When did it stop being too soon and start being too late?

When they got to the gate, Staunton put his hand into his pocket and pulled out a quarter. He gave it to Estelle. He did it carelessly, to show how little a quarter meant to him.

Owen broke a branch off the pin-cherry bush and began to strip off its leaves. They fell from his fingers, red as blood. Then Staunton got into his car, backed it out and was gone.

Owen turned to go back to the house.

Then, "Daddy," Estelle said. There was a sound in her voice that had never been there before. It was whining, self-important.

When Owen turned to look at her, she tilted her head back and hooked her thumbs into the sash at her waist. Her lower lip came out as she smiled.

"Daddy," Estelle said. "I want . . ."

She didn't get any further. Owen seized her by the arm, stopping speech.

"You try a trick like that again and I'll tan you good," he said.

Then he dropped her arm. It was as if he could not bear to touch her flesh with his. He turned his back on her and walked toward the house. But when he got to the back step, he turned again to look at her.

The child stood where he had left her. An expression, and then an expression, and then another passed across her face. The consciousness of her own importance had left her now, and she seemed curiously unprotected without it.

She stood on the path where Owen had left her. And then as he watched she turned all around, a complete circle. It was as if she was looking for somebody who ought to be there, but wasn't.

Owen watched her.

Good, he thought. *Good.*

When the alarm went off at 4 the next morning, Owen was already awake, staring into the dark. He had a headache that seemed to extend down one arm to his elbow, and something else as well — a knowledge in his bones — that made him feel heavy, swollen. But he got up and dressed in the dark of the house and then he went out into the dark outside. When he had hitched up his team, he climbed onto the rack and started out.

It wasn't like an ordinary year. The sound of wagons in the dark: ordinarily that was sound to put life into a man. But this year it was only hard wheels on hard road, and the sound of his pitchfork bump, bump, bumping on the bare floor of the rack. Owen didn't think about what might be coming. He didn't tell himself that this job was better than no job. He wasn't speaking to himself at all.

There were a dozen men sitting in the yellow light of

the lamp when he got to the Allsopps, all of them fork-
ing up beef and potatoes. There were three strangers
among them: Staunton, Elreno and a young fellow from
Ontario, a boy who had been drifting through when
Staunton hired him. The rest of the men, all of whom
had worked together before, were trying to bridge their
feeling of strangeness with the newcomers by joking.

Owen didn't join in. He didn't feel like eating but
he ate; he had to if he wanted to work. As he ate, he
took a good look at Staunton's son.

Elreno didn't look the way he would have expected
him to look. Staunton was big-bellied and Elreno was
lean. Staunton had that strange, gentle voice; Elreno
showed signs of being a loudmouth. But the most surprising thing was that Elreno had a moustache. Owen
noticed that there were no jokes about Elreno's
moustache. Nobody suggested that they would all gang
up on him in the bunkhouse some night and shave it off.

"Last year I was second-in-command," Elreno announced. "But this year I'm running the show." He
wasn't joking exactly; he wanted them to know.

The big push, Owen thought. That was what the men
would be calling Elreno in a few days.

He could see the other men sizing the Stauntons up
and coming to their own conclusions. Like Owen, not
too many of them had much to be concerned about as
far as knowing their jobs went. Do your job right and
there was nothing anybody could bawl you out about.
Owen had been threshing for ten years and he'd never
been bawled out yet. He never expected to be.

Pretty soon they finished eating. "Time to start,
boys," Staunton said. But then he remembered that
Elreno was the boss now. He turned to Elreno to let him
give the orders.

"You, Blackie," Elreno said. He was looking at Owen. "You and Stevenson can start out now. You can be first up. And Deacon and Sedgewick can follow you."

It was the first time in his life that anyone had ever called Owen *Blackie*. Before he could decide how he felt about it, Staunton spoke again. "I've never had a black working for me before," he said.

The men laughed, nervously. Owen didn't join in. He pushed himself back from the table and turned to young Bob Allsopp, who was field-pitching. "Want a ride out?" he asked.

They went into the yard then: Owen, Stevenson and Bob Allsopp. But as Owen was untying his lines, Staunton appeared at the side of his rack.

"Look," Staunton said, "I guess I shouldn't have said what I did just now."

In the gathering light, Owen saw that he looked like he meant it. "I was only making fun," Staunton said.

Owen nodded, acknowledging the apology.

Then, "Another thing," Staunton said. "I'd take it as a favour if you'd drive my team for a day or two."

For a minute, Owen didn't say anything. If he was driving Staunton's team, that meant that the young fellow from Ontario would be driving his. It was a lot to ask a man: to put his team into the hands of a boy he didn't even know.

He hesitated a moment, considering. There was the clatter of any empty rack as Stevenson started off for the field.

"It's not that my team's not broke," Staunton said. "We had them threshing last year. But the little mare never did get over being nervous around the separator. It would be better for the first few days if she had a good man driving her."

He was asking Owen as an older man, a man who knew horses, to give the boy a break. There was no way Owen could refuse.

"I'll give it a try," Owen said.

"I appreciate that," Staunton said.

So Owen tied his lines and climbed off his own rack and on to Staunton's. Staunton followed him, stopping to pat the mare on her rump. "She's a good little horse," he said. "I've never had one I liked better."

With the Allsopp boy beside him, Owen started off for the field. When he got there he headed for the south fence. Owen liked to go to the far side of a field and then work in toward the machine.

It was easy work: pitching the bundles up. The crop was thin and light and the bundles were small: about a third of the size a bundle ought to be. But the stooks were so far apart that you had a lot of walking to do. Besides that, there was a lot of loose stuff that the binder had missed. It took a long time to make a load.

Going in, Owen heard the outfit before he saw it. He came over a hill with his load and saw Staunton and Elreno standing together in front of the separator, identical sweater collars pulled high out of identical combination overalls. Stevenson was already in, pitching in bundles on the north side of the feeder.

The beginning of a straw pile was forming underneath the blower, and the first wheat formed a russet arc from grain spout to waggon box. Chaff hung suspended in the stillness of the morning. Seeing it, Owen felt the rhythm of the season reaching out to him. He wanted to get his team in there, to start pitching bundle for bundle with Stevenson.

He headed Staunton's horses in and their heads went

down and their ears went back. As they got closer to the
noise and the dust and the long flapping belts, the little
mare began to shake. Owen saw that she was the kind
of horse that would shake every time she was brought
in, all the time he was unloading. But he had no dif-
ficulty driving her in to where she was supposed to go.
It was as if she had forgotten there was any alternative.

Owen tied his lines to the linepost before he picked
up his fork. He wouldn't have bothered with his own
team but this team was different. He didn't trust them.
And tied, they couldn't run away. They couldn't pull
a waggon with their mouths.

When they were tied, he began to pitch down his load.
It was rhythmic work, keeping the feeder loaded. The
bundles, once they were on the feeder, didn't remain
bundles very long. Chains glittered and slats rattled and
the bundles jiggled up to the twine cutter. Then the curved steel blades came down and the bundles collapsed and
disappeared into the cylinder.

The second load took even longer to pick up than the
first, because he picked up most of it alone. Bob Allsopp
was off helping another man.

When he pulled in to the machine, Staunton was gone,
but Elreno was there, waiting for him. Again, the
machine was running empty on his side when he came
in.

Owen tied his lines. As he started to unload, Elreno
walked back from the tractor. He raised his voice so that
Owen could hear him over the noise of the machinery.

"Just where in hell do you think you've been?" he
demanded.

Owen looked at him, but he didn't answer. There was
no answer to a question like that. But as he pitched

bundles his resentment grew. Elreno knew how light the crop was this year. He knew how far you had to walk to get a load. And if he didn't know how much loose stuff there was to be picked up, he ought to know. Did he want you to leave the loose stuff in the field? That would give him something to holler about, wouldn't it?

But Owen knew that Elreno hadn't hollered because he was late. Elreno hollered because he believed that hollering was his right. Or else because he wanted to show everybody right from the start who was boss.

As Owen forked the last of his load onto the feeder, he saw that Frank Deacon had pulled into place behind him. And then he saw Elreno walking up to Deacon. Elreno stood beneath Deacon's rack, looking up.

"I suppose you call that a load?" he said.

Frank Deacon didn't bother to deny that his load was light. It wasn't, and Elreno knew it.

Deacon looped his lines over the linepost, climbed down the front of the rack, and faced Elreno.

"Listen, Elreno," he said. "I'm willing to settle this here and now. Find out which one of us is the better man."

Frank Deacon was a well-built man, and handy with his fists. Elreno looked at him for a minute. Then he tried to look disdainful. But then he turned and started walking back to the machine.

Looking around, Owen saw the men exchanging smiles. *Elreno went back a lot faster than he come out,* they would say later. *And a good job he did,* they would say. *Frank Deacon don't back down from nobody.*

Suddenly Owen felt again the shame there was in being small. A man ought to be big, like Frank Deacon. A man ought not to put up with things. He had put up with things, had kept his trap shut while Elreno gave him hell. He had let Staunton come into his house, had let Staunton hold his child. It seemed to Owen that Staunton and Elreno weren't really two different people at all; they were one and the same. As he and Estelle were one and the same, or had been one and the same.

But when Owen though of Estelle, the way he thought of her was as she had been on Staunton's knee: sitting quietly while Staunton pawed over her. And when he thought that, something new happened to Owen. His thoughts stopped altogether and a feeling came over him. It came over him in waves, wave on wave of it, as if it had started a long way back and built up until now it was irresistible; it had to be surrendered to.

He swung his lines, startling Staunton's team. They took off at a trot. The rack rattled and the pitchfork bumped on the bare floor, but Owen didn't hear them. He didn't think either: not about himself and Estelle, or Staunton and Elreno. It was as if he had left them all behind, himself included, back at the separator. He did not think about what had happened as he drove away to the north side of the field, beyond the place where he would encounter field pitchers or other teams. He didn't think about anything at all. He just drove the team until he had got away, behind a hill where he wouldn't see anybody, and nobody would see him.

He tied his lines. He couldn't do anything with his lines, not what needed to be done. He took a long time tying them, as if he were moving in sleep. It was very important that he do it right.

When he had finished, he moved to the back of the rack and picked up his fork. He got off the rack and went up to the team. And then he began to beat them.

Them . . . it. It was the mare's side he had come up on, and so she was the one that got it. She leapt and twisted in her harness. Beadings of blood appeared on her haunches and thighs. And then strings of blood swung in the air, red and viscous, as she twisted, trying to escape him. But he didn't let her. He didn't stop beating her until he was too tired to go on. And then he sat on the ground, and put his head on his knees, and wept.

It was a long time before he began to wonder how he would explain the blood on the mare to Mr. Staunton.

DAS ENGELEIN KOMMT
(The Little Angel Cometh)

When my sister Elsa was a baby she was an angel and my father called her das Engelein. At our house people never spoke in German. My mother would not allow it. Only my father ever did, and we children could hardly understand him. It was the fury of his life having non-German children. One of the furies. He had several. The Brotherhood of Man was another. My father loved the Brotherhood of Man with an ardent vocal passion.

He loved his daughters, too, I suppose, but they never knew it. He loved his son, and his daughters knew it. He loved him like Isaac loved his Jacob or like Abraham his Isaac. My father never sacrificed his Floydie on any altar; never even tried to. But he killed his daughters a thousand times over, and this is to be the story of the

47

last time he killed my sister Elsa in her snow-white Engelein gown, her wings spread and ready to soar at the church Christmas concert one year in the sandy, dry, hard farming district where we used to live.

It had to be in German. That whole church concert had to be in German. Some of the kids did O.K., they had mothers who hardly spoke English. In that community the fathers went out into the world and did the business and learned to speak the language of business. The mothers stayed home and plucked geese, and made quilts and perogies and babies, and crooned them to sleep with Komm' Herr Jesu, and sent them there with a few slaps to the ear if the child went unwilling.

So it was at our house, too. Except for the German and the Jesu. My mother didn't believe in either one. She had had it different at home. Her father was just as German as anybody else in that settlement but his mind had a different order. His daughter was to go to Normal School and be a teacher but she chose Papa instead. No wonder, I suppose. Papa was tall and beautiful and imposing and he courted every woman in the district atop his large white stallion, taking them for rides into the hills to show them the wood violets.

I think the violets stopped when my mother agreed to come into his kitchen, but his passions did not. At least I knew we had violin and lots of talk and booming laughter when the neighbors came, but cold lips and steel blue eyes when they left again.

It was a hard life in a lot of ways, but this is not that story. I tell it to you this way, though, because it is very hard, at fifty, to keep it going well. To keep the order. I've had too many other voices inside my head for so long and Papa bellering from his bed after Mama died and the third white stallion threw him, for tea and beef broth and a pen to write his newest order.

Papa was a difficult man. He lived for too many years. I looked after him for twenty-three of them. Mama, I think now sometimes, almost had it easy. She spoke back, you see, and the hate did not gather, black and hard and festering, around her heart as it did mine.

But I want to tell you about Elsa. I think that is what she means me to do when she comes now and stands by my side when I am writing away the blackness and drinking the coffee Papa forbade in this house because it repelled him. She has been dead forty-one years now, I counted it out today, and I suppose she has forgotten how to speak. On account of not knowing the sacred language, ha ha, I never believed it. Papa used to say it was all in German up there, a German pastor once told him.

For all those years I was careful not to care, but now I see that Elsa did not even go there. She couldn't have. The church says not, and they should be right on some things; it is too terrible otherwise to try to live.

But all those years I thought it was an accident and I'm sure Papa did, too. But I think Mama knew. I do not want to do the thinking sometimes, there is a danger in it, but I think now Mama knew because it raised a real uproar the way she went to bed and stayed there the day it happened and wouldn't even get up for the funeral.

But that's ahead of it again. I need the order. It is harder than to have it in your head and know it, this setting of it down. Once I wanted to be a writer and I read King Arthur over and over until I knew the order of telling things but now I cannot keep it straight.

It goes like this though. We always went to church. All but our mother. Papa said we had to go to church and learn the glory; it was not safe to live in this world otherwise. And the glory was only good if it came in German. It was the holy way. It was important because it had to do with Christus and the angels and your holy German soul. The words you spoke in the old tongue, he said, helped to get you the glory.

That pastor, I knew him, said so and Papa believed him, but our mother didn't. She said it was a peasant's attitude and it was either all true in any language or it was not all true and maybe none of it true and so what, it didn't put bread on the table, but you sure couldn't break it up into German and English and French, it wasn't logical.

And Papa said what was logical was if she would allow his daughters to speak German at the supper table but the Schroeders seemed to be such English boot lickers it seemed to be more than a man could expect to have the old tongue spoken around his own fireside. And our mother said, seemed to her it was Schroeder money bought the coal to keep the fire going in it. And Papa said Yes, yes, rub it in; and he took his box full of blue socialist tracts and saddled his white stallion with the red wild eyes and rode to Elmyra Bitner's to discuss the Brotherhood of Man.

And Mama would scrub hard at the fading red apples on the oilcloth on the kitchen table and make mouths at the way the corners were wearing through and she'd say, Come on girls, we'll make brown sugar fudge tonight.

And our mother made brown sugar fudge with butter and walnuts most nights he did that. And sometimes

when my sister Elsa peered too long into the night from
the kitchen window straining to see his white stallion
coming back out of the dark night my mother would say,
Don't be silly, girl, do you think a bear will get him or
something, he's only gone to get educated, come on and
we'll make ourselves some popcorn.

But Elsa wouldn't. She just turned her back on our
mother and went and rearranged Papa's pipes neatly
beside the family picture taken when there was only Papa
and our mother and Elsa and me because our sister
Laura already lived just at Grampa Schroeder's, she had
to, Papa said she was not his child. I hope that is the
order. It seems to fit here. Laura is important; she got
lost in a different way. And while Elsa looked at herself
being an Engelein in the family picture on the sideboard
our mother and I would pop popcorn, shelling it first,
plink-plank into a pan off the cob, and heating the heavy
frying pan on the back of the stove while we did.

Not Floydie, though. Floydie was a boy and anyway
he was young and fast asleep by that time of night. But
Elsa would only pick away at her bowlful now and again
and when Mama said, Come on, eat up, it's just the
way you like it, Elsa would get that tight look around
her eyes and say, No, I'm saving it for Floydie. And
Mama would say, He's spoiled enough, and Elsa would
say, you don't like anybody, do you? And she'd go back
to the window and look some more for Papa and his stallion and she only left her place when Floydie cried and
then she always ran to him before Mama could go.

And yet Floydie was the reason, I don't care, why Elsa
had to look out into the dark night for Papa with her
pink barn-goose eyes that got teary from too much watching. And Floydie was the reason Grampa Schroeder got

so mad he kept giving our mother money to buy us girls
new dresses for the school picnic and the church concert.
Floydie was Papa's Sunny Boy Cereal and Elsa used to
be his Engelein, but now she was just a girl who had
grown a long Schroeder neck and couldn't do arithmetic.

She couldn't learn her German piece, either. For the
church Christmas concert you had to learn to speak a
piece in German, no matter what. You had to or your
folks were shamed for ever. Even my mother went to
the church Christmas concert. It was called the Tannenbaum and nobody missed going. It was holy, and not
even the littlest ones expected to see Santa.

It was as if to say the white light of Jesu shone those
nights. The church was lit with candles. Not even the
coal oil lamps were lit and certainly not the gas mantel
lanterns with their piercing twin eyes. Only candles were
holy.

And that year, that last year, Elsa said she wanted
to be an angel. An angel in German yet, and with
twenty-eight lines to speak. When Pastor asked who
would take the part Elsa's hand shot up and it surprised me. Elsa was not that way. She would rather not
speak, even in English, and to do anything in German
killed her.

Especially speak to Papa. When you have been an
Engelein and aren't any longer, to stand before Papa
and say ihr Kinderlein kommet, zur Bethlehem Stall into
his pale slough-ice eyes doesn't help to make the wings
grow, and if you are one to have had the wings clipped
you know this is the right order to say it.

Ki*n*derlein, not Ki*d*derlein, Papa told her. *Bah*-tlah-
hem, not Bethlehem; what do you want to put a thuh
in it for? The people will think you're not raised right.

Now start the first verse again from the beginning and stand straight and speak it right. Twenty-eight lines only, a big girl like you, and you can't even learn it.

Hellslanzendem was the word that did it. Hellzadem, Elsa said. Who wouldn't? It's hard in German to get all the zeds and enns and urrs in, and lots of times the Germans don't even care when they talk it. But when it comes to their kids, watch out, they're supposed to all speak like preachers.

I talked German in my head all the time. Nobody knew it. One of the voices in my head was a German man and he told jokes sometimes in German on the pastor when church went on too long. Hier ist mir ein alter Fart, he'd say sometimes, and I would try not to smile; to smile was dangerous. And the voice would tell me to go look up Fart in Papa's German dictionary when we got home. But we never touched Papa's books, that was dangerous, too, and I would have if I'd wanted but I didn't want to care about it.

Elsa cared too much. It was dangerous. Day by day she sewed on her Engelein costume, looking quite often at the picture on the sideboard. She sewed in the parlour where you weren't supposed to use thread because it worked itself into the carpet. Mama told her she could sit there when she caught her sewing at four o'clock in the morning once by the kitchen lamp. Its flame flickered pale and yellow.

Silly goose, Mama told her, it's too hard on the eyes and I could do it on the machine in a minute. But Elsa only turned her back on Mama, pretending she was looking for the scissors, and said I want to do it. And she'd show Papa after supper how it was coming and he'd say yes, yes, but you're not gonna spend your life in a dress

53

factory, how's the piece coming? and Elsa would stand there and speak, one angel wing drooping. Bei des Lichtleins hellzadem she'd get to and Papa would look up quick and say hellslanz-, hellslanz-, put the zed in it; how come you can't remember; people will think you aren't raised right.

And then he'd call Floydie to him for a game of clap-handies and Mama would say from the parlour door, Come work in the kitchen, the light's better. But Elsa would take her piece out of her apron pocket where she kept it to learn even in the toilet, I saw her once, and her mouth made the words but she did not say them out loud and she watched Papa and Floydie whenever they laughed until Papa said, You could likely learn better in the kitchen. And then she folded her piece up and put it in her pocket and went.

And on the Tannenbaum night she spoke it pretty well, so I don't know why Papa had to do it. The candles were lit in the church and you could almost smell the glory and people shook hands with everybody they could reach even after they got sitting down in the pews, the fat ones straining hard over their chests to shake with ones sitting behind them.

Grown-ups even shook with two-year-olds, and graced each other fröhliche Weinachts whether they were mad at each other or not. And you could smell the Jap oranges from the brown paper bags, each one packed two man's hands full of peanuts and almonds and striped Christmas candy made into curlicues almost the size and shape of Floydie's new bow tie, and each one with two Jap oranges at the bottom so that you had to dig through all the other good stuff if you wanted to eat them first. One thing, Germans never were stingy when it was nuts and candy and they had the money.

Only we were never allowed to open our bags until
we got home. In our family we were never allowed, that
was Papa's way, you weren't supposed to look anxious,
it meant you weren't raised right. But that night we girls
were wearing our new dresses Grampa Schroeder had
given the money for and Floydie looked like a prince,
true enough, like Papa said, in his royal blue breeches
and snow white shirt with the ruffles. And Mama looked
nice and came along to the concert and people graced
her, too, and only a few made remarks like Well at least
we see you at Christmas. So it was all good, very good,
for once, and Elsa spoke up, spoke right up Ihr Kinderlein kommet only with not enough zeds and enns in it.
But she spoke clear and good, her eyes shining and her
hands folded and looking up into the candelabra so that
her eyes got to be two candles, too. But the trouble was,
her one wing drooped because she would not let Mama
help her sew.

And Mrs. Elmyra Bitner said afterwards to Papa, Now
Floydie, you tell that wife of yours I got time on my hands
I could help her next Chrissmas with the kids's costumes
if she wants. And Mama was standing right there, right
there beside her, and Mrs. Elmyra Bitner turned to her
next and graced her and maybe never even knew her,
Mama hardly ever came to church, but Mama said later
she did.

And Papa said it didn't matter; why worry about a
little thing like that, the point was people thought his
kids weren't raised right, how come she let the kid show
up with a costume like that, it wasn't the first time,
either. We were on the way home and the horses' hooves
sounded crisp-crunch on the hard-packed snow of the
road and the traces jingled like bells although Papa wasn't

a one to put brass bells on the harness like a lot of men did, he said it was frippery. And I tried to think hard about the Jap oranges and how they'd be when we got home and Papa let us open our bags. I had to think hard hard about them; to think about Elsa's drooping wings was too dangerous.

But when we got home and Papa had carried Floydie inside, and us girls and Mama had our coats off, Elsa wouldn't even open her bag. And Mama was undressing Floydie fast asleep on the kitchen table, and Mama had one eye on Elsa sitting silent on a hard chair by the Quebec heater with her piece in her hand, and Mama looked real nice, very nice, she hardly ever dressed up.

And Papa came up behind her, his fur coat and hat still on because he still had to go out and do the horses. And he laid his hand on Mama's shoulder and said, It's always better after church. And he showed his hard white even teeth under his silky smooth moustache, he was a very good looker always. And Mama just picked Floydie up and walked out from under his hand and said over her shoulder, Elmyra Bitner has lots of time on her hands I hear.

And Papa turned quick to the door and stepped on the paper bag with the costumes in it, I guess I should not have left it there. And he kicked at the bag and it split and the Engelein costume got tangled in his church overshoes and he grabbed it and threw it in the corner and didn't even bother putting on his barn boots because he knew he wasn't going to the barn, I guess. And he drove out the yard, and the harness traces clanging no rhythm, no whatsoever rhythm, because the horses were going too hard, and it was cold for their lungs to go hard. Like Grampa Schroeder said, Papa was not much good on horses.

And Mama came out of the bedroom and picked up
the Engelein costume and said, Never mind, Grampa
said you looked real pretty. And Elsa grabbed the
costume out of her hands and scrunched it all up tight
and held it to her and went to the window to strain her
eyes into the night to see Papa going.

And there was no moon.

And that night, before Papa got home from Elmyra
Bitner's, Elsa took the key to the box stall and went in
to the stallion. And Papa found her when he got home.
And afterwards he would not even sell the stallion.

And when we moved to town a little later because
Grampa Schroeder said so and even bought the house,
he kept it at Elmyra Bitner's and went out from town
Sundays to go to German church and ride his snow white
stallion.

The words are said. The words of Elsa's dying are
now said. They are in order I think and it does not seem
too dangerous to have them down on paper. And Elsa
does not speak yet, but I somehow think, now the words
are all in order, if I just sit here and do not rearrange
them, and think very hard on Papa, that she will nod
and go.

Sharon Butala

O WHAT VENERABLE AND REVEREND CREATURES

"He said it was a heart attack," Meredith said. She couldn't seem to fit the phone receiver onto the cradle. "He said she was bringing dessert to the table and she started to stagger. She sat down and then she said, 'Oh,' and fell over." Meredith suddenly let go of the receiver and balled the napkin she had been holding, pressing it against her face, trying to stifle the noise she could hear herself making. She heard Bill move, felt his arm go around her, felt his hand smoothing her hair.

"Poor girl," he said. "Poor girl."

There was a rustling in the doorway. Stacey. Stacey would have to be told. Meredith wiped her eyes with the napkin and stood back from Bill, who had turned to the door. Stacey leaned against the door frame, one hand raised to her shoulder, the thin, nicotine-stained fingers twisting a lock of thick, curly brown hair that hung uncombed, in a mass around her shoulders. Her eyes glittered. The petulance of her expression made her look younger than eighteen.

"Who was that?" she asked, looking at the phone rather than them. Even when she was in a rage, or coldly withdrawn from them, she could not change the startling depth and resonance of her voice. It was the voice of a great stage actress.

"Your Grandpa Robertson," Bill said. "Your grandmother is dead." Meredith put her hand on Bill's arm.

"About two hours ago," she said to her daughter, and tried to think of something to add that might comfort Stacey, knowing at the same time the absolute futility of this. Stacey's expression, held so carefully false for so long, had wavered, and she took a step into the room, staring at her mother, her eyes widening, deepening into some infinite vision of horror.

"Oh," she said. "Oh." Meredith put her hand out to Stacey, who, remembering herself, stiffened theatrically and made as though to back away.

Bill said, suddenly impatient, "We can get the first flight west in the morning. I'll start making arrangements." He patted Meredith's shoulder, then skirted the table, passed Stacey, and paused in the doorway. "You'd better start packing, Stacey," he said. "You're coming, too." Meredith could see the abrupt shine of sweat on Stacey's neck as she lifted her chin. They watched her, Bill indifferent, no longer even amused; Meredith sadly, seeing how beautiful she was, like some spoiled, decadent rich child in the movies; her lush hair, her fine, delicate nose, the dark shadows under her eyes, the hysteria prickling just beneath her skin.

"You must be out of your mind," Stacey said. She shoved her hands into her jeans' pockets, lifted her chin, and turned toward the door. Bill didn't move, blocking it with his big, square body. He stood looking down at his daughter.

"I can't get away from school," she said finally, her voice rising, a tremor creeping in. "You were so damn anxious for me to go back, and now . . ."

"I know it's semester break," he interrupted. His voice was tight, his bitterness barely covered. "I know you failed all three courses. The school called my office. They can't see any point in your coming back for another semester. You're just wasting everybody's time, they said."

Standing behind Stacey, Meredith saw, beneath the sharp points of her shoulder blades, the thin cloth of her shirt quivering minutely. She closed her eyes. Stacey four, five, six years old, body arched, eyes rolled back, screaming in terror, smiling in the morning as if there were no blackness, no endless night.

"Start packing," Bill said. "We are all going to your grandmother's funeral." Stacey twisted one shoulder and slid past him without speaking.

In the morning they boarded a plane, Bill in his three-piece grey suit, Meredith in her aging but still smart blue Chanel, and Stacey, rumpled and sleepy, her hair uncombed, wearing fraying faded jeans and a stained brown windbreaker. They flew west with Stacey seated several rows behind them, stilting their conversation and poisoning Meredith's grief with her hostility, which they could feel boring through the rows of seats separating them.

At Regina they rented a car and drove west for another four hours, soon leaving the wide paved highway for roads that grew narrower and more and more treacherous under their burden of ice and snow. Meredith had not been home in over a year. She was a rancher's daughter, but she had lived the last twenty years in Toronto, and for the last fifteen she had taught chemistry at the university. Each time she returned home she was grateful that she had escaped the hardship, the male chauvinism, the ignorance.

The small church was full even though there was a blizzard blowing outside. Her father had begun to stoop and to move more slowly. After the service, stepping out of the church into the swirling snow, he hesitated and looked around in a bewildered way, blinking, as though he was surprised to find himself still in the town of his birth.

At the cemetery, high on the hillside, the wind whipped blasts of snow across the rectangular hole in the ground and made their heavy coats flap against their legs. Stacey had refused to get out of the car, although Meredith did not notice this till later. The minister hurried through the ceremony, his words lost in the storm.

The next day Bill went back East, leaving Stacey and Meredith behind to look after Meredith's father for a week or two, "until he gets back on his feet."

At breakfast, when Meredith served him his bacon and eggs, her father put his arm around her and said, "You're a good girl, Merry. Never gave us a moment's trouble. Who'd ever think I'd have a professor for a daughter." Meredith kissed his forehead and sat down across from him. "Your mother and me," he said carefully, as if he was trying out the sound of it, "your

mother and me,'' he repeated, stronger this time, ''we
. . .'' He seemed to have forgotten what he had started
to say.

''Maybe now you'll think about retirement,'' Meredith said.

''Yeah,'' he said. He stirred his coffee. ''You and
Stacey could chase the cows around to the feed ground
this morning,'' he said. ''You know, like you used to.
It's too damn cold for them to go without feed.''

''All right,'' Meredith said. ''It'll be good for Stacey
to have something to do.''

After her father had gone out to the barn, Meredith
knocked on Stacey's door. At home she had given up
waking Stacey in the mornings. When she came home
at night Stacey would be gone and Meredith would hear
her coming in at three or four in the morning, making
noise so she and Bill would wake and know how late it
was.

''Wake up, Stacey,'' she called. ''Your grandpa needs
us. We have to give him a hand.'' Silence. ''Stacey?''
she said, opening the door. The curtains were closed but
she could make out Stacey lying on her back staring at
the ceiling. Her clothes were strewn on the floor. The
room had a musty, closed-in smell.

After a moment Stacey threw back the covers and sat
on the side of the bed. Meredith went back to the kitchen. Soon Stacey came in, wearing the same jeans and
shirt she had worn since the funeral. Her hair needed
washing and there was sleep in the corners of her eyes.

''What?'' Stacey asked.

''We have to chase the cattle away from the riverbed
up onto the feed grounds.'' Stacey was staring through
the window at the outdoor thermometer.

"It's twenty below out there!" she said. "You must be nuts!"

"I am not nuts," Meredith said, banging the coffee pot. "When it's very cold like this, they go down into all the nooks and crannies along the riverbed looking for shelter." She poured Stacey a cup of coffee without looking at her. "And then they don't hear the tractor, or see the feed coming and they miss it." She put the coffee pot back on the stove. "They can't endure the cold without good feed and they die." She tried to smile at Stacey. "So it is essential that we go out and chase them up. It's only about a mile and a half."

"Christ!" Stacey said, but Meredith had seen the welling brightness in her eyes and knew nothing would stop her from going, from trying the bitter air in her lungs, from testing the feel of the thigh-deep snow, from challenging a twelve-hundred pound range cow or grovelling in panic in front of one.

On the third morning Stacey rose without being called. She came into the kitchen where Meredith, already wearing most of her outdoor clothes, was hurrying to get the dishes washed before she went out. Stacey poured herself a cup of coffee, not answering her mother's good morning, and stood looking out the window.

"You don't need to go out this morning," she said. Her voice was husky, as though she hadn't spoken for weeks. "I know what to do."

"I don't mind," Meredith said.

"I can do it!" Stacey said. "Meredith," she added, rolling the r. Meredith flushed but didn't speak. Stacey put on her parka and went outside. Meredith could hear her whistling for the dogs.

When the dishes were done, the beds made, and a pie

in the oven, Stacey still had not returned. I'll bet she's romping in the snow with the dogs, Meredith thought, or maybe examining those caves along the riverbank, now over-hung with tongues of ice that had kept safe foxes or young coyotes through her own childhood.

It surprised and pleased her to think that Stacey might be having fun. A creature of contradictions, paradoxes and extremes, Stacey possibly did not even know what fun was. Whenever the police brought her back after she had run away, (and then seemed not to know what to do with herself, or even why she had gone), she always looked so pale and sickly that Meredith could only pity her, for the demon that pursued her and would not give her peace.

She decided to clean Stacey's room for her as a way of thanking her for saving her from the long, tiring walk through the deep snow on the riverbottom. She stripped her bed and put clean sheets on it and put away the discarded clothes. Stacey's suitcase was still lying on the floor. Meredith picked it up by the handle intending to set it upright in the closet, but as she lifted it, it fell open, spilling the contents. Oh no, Meredith thought. She'll accuse me of snooping. Quickly she bent over and began to replace the tangled underwear and cotton shirts. A plastic bag fell out on the floor. As she bent to pick it up she saw that it was plumped full of something that looked like dried grass. Marijuana.

I might have known, she thought. Stacey the trouble-maker, the eternal embarrassment, the albatross she and Bill wore around their necks. How could she do such a thing? How could she bring this into her grandparents' house at a time like this? She went to the kitchen and looked out the window. Stacey was crossing the yard,

snow clinging to her pants, to her thighs, the dogs jumping at her side.

She came into the house, stamping the snow off her
boots, and throwing back her hood. Meredith stood in
the doorway of the kitchen facing her, holding the bag
chest high in front of her. Stacey looked at it. For a moment she said nothing. Then she said, ''Snooping
again?'' and grabbed for the bag. Meredith jerked it out
of her reach and stepped back into the kitchen.

''How could you do this?'' she asked.

''It's only grass, Meredith,'' Stacey said. ''It's no big
deal. How could you do this?'' She mimicked her
mother.

Meredith reached out, she did not know she was going
to do this, and slapped Stacey across the face. They stared
at each other. Stacey's face drained white, the red slap
mark standing out like a birthmark. Meredith's palm
stung.

The bag of marijuana had fallen to the floor. Neither
of them bent to pick it up. Stacey's eyes began to fill
with tears. Two large drops gathered at the bottom of
each eye and as Meredith watched, they spilled over and
began to run down Stacey's cheeks.

''You have caused me so much pain,'' Meredith said.
She bent and picked up the bag, took it to the half-bath
which was by the back door, emptied it into the toilet
and flushed it. Stacey still had not moved. Meredith
began to shake. She waited for the screams, the attack,
the fainting.

There was a thumping on the step outside the door and
then Meredith's father called, opening the door,
''Somebody give me a hand here.'' Meredith quickly
pulled back the door. He was struggling into the house,

66

half-pushing, half-carrying a slick reddish creature ahead
of him. Stacey gasped and put her hand over her mouth.

"It's a new calf, sweetheart," her grandfather said,
laughing. If he saw the red mark or the tears, he gave
no sign.

"Is it alive?" Stacey asked. "Ugh! It's all slimy!" Her
grandfather put the calf down on the hall floor with a
thump.

"Got to get it warmed up," he said. "Or it'll die."

"What are you doing, dad, calving in January?"
Meredith asked. She was surprised at how ordinary her
voice sounded.

"Goddamn bulls must have got in with the heifers last
spring. I found this one near the feed grounds, just
born."

"Heifer okay?" Meredith asked, as if she had never
left.

"Yeah, that one's all right, but I found another dead
one north. Calving too long. I didn't know they'd been
bred. You can't tell with heifers, and now look at the
mess. Its ears are frozen."

"The cord's frozen too," Meredith said. Behind her,
Stacey made a 'yuck' sound. Again Meredith was surprised that Stacey was still there.

"It'll be safe in the half-bath till it gets warm and dry,"
he said. "I didn't dare leave it for the mother to lick
it off." He turned to the door. "There's bound to be
more," he said. "I have to go check the rest of the herd.
Keep an eye on it, Merry," he said. "You too, Stacey."
He went outside. Stacey knelt, ignoring Meredith, coo-
ing to the calf.

In the late afternoon he came back to the house carrying another calf. Meredith was reading in the living

room. When she went to the kitchen she saw Stacey on her hands and knees in the bathroom trying to dry the calf off with Meredith's blow dryer. Her grandfather was kneeling beside her and they were talking. Meredith left the room quickly before either of them saw her.

Every morning Stacey chased the cattle down the riverbed and when she finished that, she went up to the feed grounds and helped her grandfather and his hired man fork the hay off the flat deck to the waiting cows. After that, the three of them came in for the noon meal which Meredith had prepared, and then, leaving the dishes for Meredith, they went down to the barn to help the new calves nurse. Stacey did not answer when Meredith spoke to her. The days dragged by.

Late one afternoon Meredith's father came hurrying in.

"Jim and I have to take that steer with water belly to the vet," he said. "We should be back by seven. I got a heifer due to calve in the barn so I have to get back as soon as I can."

Stacey ate her supper in front of the television set in the living room while Meredith ate at her place in the kitchen.

At eight o'clock Meredith's father had still not returned. The temperature had dropped to thirty below and the wind was rising. She supposed he was storm-stayed somewhere. After a lifetime in this country, she reassured herself, he won't take chances, he'll know how to take care of himself. Remembering the heifer, she put on her parka and went down to the barn. It had begun to calve. She could see one tiny hoof protruding from beneath the upraised tail. She studied the heifer nervously. She couldn't tell if it had been trying to deliver for a long time or not. Oh, Lord, she thought. What will I do? She decided to wait an hour before she tried to help and with luck, by then her father might be back.

At nine o'clock she went back to the barn. Now she could see both hooves. That's too slow, she said to herself. I'm pretty sure that's too slow. We'll have to help her. I wish dad would get home. She struggled back to the house, the fur-trimmed hood of her parka pulled well around her face, her hands thrust up the opposite sleeves.

"Stacey," she said to her daughter, who had not taken her eyes off the television.

"What?" Stacey said, still not looking at her.

"That heifer can't deliver on her own, and your grandfather's not back, and . . . we'll have to pull it."

"Pull it yourself," Stacey said.

"I can't, Stacey," Meredith cried. "I'm not strong enough. You have to help me. I can't do it alone." To her amazement, tears were running down her cheeks. She wiped them off and then stared at the wet streak on her hand. Stacey was watching her now, that brightness back in her eyes. "Please help me, Stacey," she said. "The heifer will die if we don't pull her calf. And the calf will die right away if we don't get it out of there." Stacey's eyes, wide, bright and hard, had shifted away from Meredith to some invisible thing. Her mouth was open, she was almost smiling. She rose and went to the kitchen, with Meredith following, and put on her parka, boots and mittens.

The weather had been getting steadily worse. When they opened the back door, it blew out of their hands and banged against the wall. They had to walk backwards to the barn; the wind, bitterly cold now, was blowing into their faces with such force.

"Well, where is she?" Stacey asked when they were inside the barn. Meredith pointed. The cow raised her head and mooed. Stacey went to her and stared at the little pair of hooves. "How do we pull it?" she asked.

"This is all I know how to do," Meredith said. She picked a rope hanging from a nail on the frosted barn wall. It had a loop on one end. She went to the heifer and set the loop over the two protruding hooves and tightened it. "Take the end." She held onto the rope in front of Stacey. "Pull," she said. Nothing happened. The heifer mooed again. "Pull!" Meredith grunted. "One, two, three!" They pulled so hard that when the calf came, in one welcome whoosh, they fell backward into the straw on top of each other.

"We did it!" Stacey said, standing up and looking at the calf.

"I bet it weighs close to a hundred pounds," Meredith said. They took the rope off the calf and stood back, their white breaths fading in the air above their faces. "I don't know how we're going to get it to the house, especially in that wind."

"It'll freeze to death if we don't," Stacey said. She pushed open the barn door, and each taking one end of the calf, staggering with its weight, floundering in the drifts, falling, being pushed off course and blinded by the wind-driven snow, they got the calf to the house. It had taken them fifteen minutes to go a hundred yards. They put the calf in the bathroom and Meredith turned up the thermostat.

"It looks okay," Stacey said, dubiously.

"At least, not any worse than the others did," Meredith answered. "I'll put some coffee on." Was her father safe somewhere? "I hope dad gets home soon," she said.

Stacey was rubbing her reddened hands together, blowing on her fingers and sniffing.

They turned on the television set and sat drinking coffee in the warm living room. Now and then the calf in the bathroom bleated and made a knocking noise with its hooves as it tried to stand on the slippery vinyl.

"I can just imagine the mess in there," Meredith said. Stacey laughed. Suddenly Meredith realized that she had not been watching Stacey, she had been only looking at her, as one person looks at another during a conversation. It had been years, years, since she had simply talked to Stacey, since she had been able to forget that this was her disturbed, delinquent child who couldn't be trusted, who had to be watched. Now she noticed that Stacey had put on a little weight, she was not quite so painfully thin and her skin was less yellowish. Stacey had lit a cigarette and was lounging in the chair, laughing at something on the screen. Her socks were dirty, her jeans worn out and clumsily patched, her cotton shirt thin and faded and she wore no bra under it.

Meredith had a sense of the shadows around the edges of the room darkening, of Stacey's form taking on a depth, a richness of colour, another dimension that made her real and powerful, like the central figure in a Rembrandt.

Do I really love her? Meredith asked herself. She remembered what the school psychologist had said when Stacey was fourteen and had been caught in the boys' bathroom with five or six boys.

"I think, Mrs. Wallace, that some kids are already lost." Her hair was greying, she would soon retire. "I've been at this work a long time. I know I shouldn't say this to you. But I think some kids are lost. From the moment they breathe on their own, they're lost. I don't know why it should be that way." She had looked very old. Meredith could hardly believe that this was the same woman who stood up at community meetings and gave speeches about you and your teenager. "Take her to a psychiatrist." That was all she would say.

When Meredith had asked the psychiatrist for some word, for some explanation, he had said only, "No one is responsible for what Ortega called 'this terrible reality.' " Meredith did not know what he had meant.

Do I really love her? she asked herself again.

She had been an ordinary baby, her brown eyes alert and intelligent, quick to smile, and when she could walk she had been into everything like all babies. She was slightly underweight at birth, she cried a lot, Meredith had worked all through her childhood, but none of these things, not together, not singly, accounted for Stacey. Nothing accounted for Stacey.

They stayed up to watch the late movie and during it both Stacey and Meredith fell asleep. The next time Meredith looked at her watch, it was six o'clock. Her father, still wearing his snowmobile suit, was looking down at her.

"Had to sleep in the truck till it cleared," he said. He sat down heavily in a chair and unzipped his suit. "I'm getting too old for this," he said. "I'm going to have to cut back on my herd come spring. I don't know how I'd have managed without you two this last couple of weeks."

He had grown old since her last visit. He was an old man. He couldn't be left alone. She was his only relative, the only one to manage the burden of his life. But it would be impossible for him to live in the city. In the

city, staying with them, he would die. She should stay
here and look after him.

He had leaned back. His eyes were closed and sadness
wrapped around him like a cloak. I should stay, she
thought. Snow was banked up around the picture window and the stars were still out.

"I hate to leave you, dad," she said, her mouth dry,
"but I have to get back to my job, to Bill."

"I know, I know," her father said. He looked across
to the window as though to hide his despair from her.
One way or another, she thought, our children all break
our hearts. It is the way things are.

Stacey, lying on the couch near them, stirred and they
both turned to her. She sat up and they saw that she
had been awake through their talk. Her face was lit with
an internal light, her voice beautiful.

"I'm staying," she said. Meredith and her father
watched her, and Meredith opened her mouth to speak.
"It's my life," Stacey said to her. She looked back to
her grandfather. "I'm staying."

Meredith's father drove her to town, where she caught
a bus to Regina, and from Regina, a plane to Toronto.
It was a flight that had originated in Vancouver and the
plane was full. A young mother and her four-year-old
boy sat beside Meredith. The child was restless, sitting
on his mother's knee at the window, asking for water,
asking to go to the bathroom, whining for a toy.

"I don't know what to do with him," the young
woman said apologetically to Meredith. Meredith
thought, I could tell her that he's not bothering me, or
that he will probably grow up to be a Prime Minister,
or at least a decent, normal adult.

Instead, she said, "He's a handsome child, and he

seems quite bright.'' After a while she said, ''I have a daughter; she's grown up now. She was a beautiful baby, lots of dark hair and big brown eyes, and always asking questions, too. She used to love to throw bread to the pigeons in the park. She wasn't at all afraid of them. They would come closer and closer and she would stand still, her little arm outstretched with the bread in her hand. They would take it out of her fingers and how that delighted her. Once, one perched on her shoulder and she smiled, there was such wonder in her smile and her eyes.''

But the little boy was squirming again, he had climbed from his seat and was banging a toy car against the window. His mother held his arm to stop him and he began to wail. The young woman was not listening to Meredith. But Meredith hardly noticed. She leaned back in her seat and closed her eyes. She thought about Stacey in the park with the pigeons.

Beverly Harris

THE SOMA BUILDING

I was born on November 7, the anniversary of the Bolshevik Revolution, and it has always seemed impossible to me that I could have been born on any other day. The right time is a resting place. November 7 does not seem arbitrary; November 7 is home. And yet I have been told that my father took to his bed on the day that I was born. They say he ''took to his bed'' as if there were a magnetic, perhaps even sexual, attraction between them. Had he arrived home (did he even go?) after witnessing what had issued from my mother's body (blue apparently, though they rescued me in time) and wanted himself to return to the birthing bed? To close himself up in a world before his world began? It was always, after that time, *his* bed, never my mother's. I suppose she did go there at night (there were no extra beds) and lie down beside my father and go to sleep, but it was never *her* bed, or *their* bed, but *his* bed. From November 7, 1946 on, my mother was only a visitor to it.

In the daytime my father stretched out down the middle of it, the brown metal headboard curving up around the back of his head protectively. The blankets managed the rest — grey rough things with faded candy stripes on the border. He stayed and stayed. It wasn't death, it was arrival, wonder at his own arrival, arrival again and again, and fear of finding out about departure. When I arrived, he arrived *again*.

He seldom got up, lying there in the tall narrow room at the back of our house all the years I was growing up. ''Go and ask your father when he would like his lunch'': my mother was overweight, with a red face when she bustled with meals, and kind. My father took women in his room (my mother right in the kitchen wiping the lunch crumbs off the tabletop), getting their names from the telephone book I have been told, seducing them with his impeccable French. They were healthy women at first as I recall, pretty or artistic, *interesting,* but as my father got older and weaker (he was extremely thin by the '50s and one lung had collapsed), the lady friends that came to see him were progressively wheezy and/or drunk. People begin to live their lives with intentions of purposeful and fruitful goals: perhaps my father had wanted to become a principal actor in a larger scene.

My mother found another man eventually, a man who painted meticulous landscapes. I remember her best off to lakesides with him on his motorcycle, clamped to his back like the empty canvas, her wispy curls threatening grey in the grey weather.

Who wants to live the way they lived? But what did

I do in that room in the Soma building that spring? A few pages which did not seem to make a successful story. Allan, the fellow in the next office who made architectural models, told me that the date set for the demolition of the building was Hallowe'en, 1984. I recognized that as a fascinating piece of information and even typed it out so I could stare at it. Could I, I wondered over and over, make something of this fact? Could I weave it into the story, use it to show that . . . to show what? I didn't know; I tried, but I couldn't infuse it with significance. It sat as a note on a page, unconnected. I wanted to join it with myself, with Allan and his grids of plastic buildings and foam and wire trees pinned down beside them.

I could have gone into Allan's room any time and studied his models and then related their perfect world and its significance to my story. I could even have used Allan as the model for my main character because the fact that he is a model-maker was perfect for a story. Was that why I came to that room in that building — to make things cohere, to write a coherent story? Perhaps I did not stay long enough, moving out after only a few months. All my belongings were packed and out in the van and yet I remember stubbornly standing there in that old building, staring out the window thinking of the words I had typed about the demolition. Hallowe'en, 1984: I failed to make it cohere.

My father taught me to play chess behind closed doors. Those were the loneliest afternoons, when the summer streets were deserted, when all my friends were gone, when the dandelion seeds wafted by the upstairs window, leaving their whiteness on the screen. The world had departed its houses, the shafts of hot dull sunlight

falling on no one. You could yell, but to whom? The
wooden men had felt bottoms that made no sound as
they slipped from red to black square. One square and
another, diagonally or forwards in a straight line. They
faced me always with the most frighteningly dead
acknowledgement: knight, bishop, queen. They defeated
me. It was a game into which I entered blindly and which
snapped shut behind me. I grew up there.

My father once said to me, anyone is as happy as
anyone else. It has been my most difficult task, trying
to convince myself otherwise, to convince myself that
I am entitled to happiness, perhaps great happiness.
When my father said this, he was running the elevator
at the Douglas Psychiatric Hospital. It was a job he took
to get him out and he lasted there several months. He
stood there for hours pressing the Hold button while the
insane bent in and out in paper slippers. To me at the
time (this was in the late '60s), this mechanical activity
seemed incomprehensibly beneath his great intelligence,
but I can see now the comfort it may have provided him,
and rest from his inconclusions. The elevator slipped up
and down the shaft, filling and emptying, opening and
closing, while time went on past it. Up to the seventh
floor and down to the fifth: variations within the absolute-
ly known. He wore the blue wool cardigan I had knit
for him several years earlier, nice, except that the left side
of it hung down farther than the right. I had made a
miscalculation on the number of stitches and it just
drooped, so sad. Whenever I saw it, I wanted to start
my whole life over again. There was a time (and
sometimes even now I find myself lapsing into it) when
all my mistakes seemed to rise up all around me like
buildings.

I thought that I would buy a bird and a bird cage (wicker perhaps), but I never did. I thought that the bird would be happy and, if I were lucky, sing out from time to time unexpectedly in the emptiness of that high-ceilinged room I tried to fill with words. But the time went, miraculously, by. It was the room in which I was to take my life in my hands, it was the dream I dreamed of a room to put my life into, and out of, like a jar.

Pride persuades many that life can be lived according to their own plans, my father wrote as he sat in the *Bungalow Grill,* a restaurant he went to once in a while at Sherbrooke and Belgrave. When the weather was perfect (which, for him, was not more than a few days a year), he managed to set out to the corner on foot, a stooping skeletal figure, six feet tall, dressed in an old suit jacket and peaked wool cap. He stopped frequently to catch his breath and estimate the remaining steps to his destination. When he arrived, he ordered a cup of tea and opened his notebook to write. I have suspected for some time, he wrote, that most of the answers to mental illness are answers to life itself. And: there come sometimes those moments of indecision as I try going out. And: one of the problems I face in writing this is the urge to try and write on several different subjects or events at the same time. And: my own anxiety has been caused by some form of greed — the unbalanced desire for something to which I have no right.

It is with these bits of his writing that I have become obsessed. So many times I have tried to find the key to them. And yet the things that I consider significant in my own life have so often been merely isolated and floating fragments, disconnections. To prove a point, to make an argument coherent, has sometimes seemed impossible. They say that Clara Schumann loved Brahms for forty years: today this seems of immense importance. Today I have decided that if I were ever to write a novel, the children would be called Bonnie, Jasper and Paully: this, too, seems important. Last week a man I hadn't seen in five years spilled a whole cup of coffee on himself when I sat down beside him in the restaurant: I am not sure yet if this is important. Some days I am afraid, some days I am unafraid.

I rented an empty office room in the Soma Building on Eighth Avenue in the spring of 1981. I bought a desk that I thought in the dim light of the second-hand furniture store was wood and found later not to be so. I unloaded my books onto shelves, hung up a few plants, and thought I would write a story. I wrote a story about a man who could not understand his wife, although he loved her very much. In fact, one of the reasons he loved her so much was that he didn't understand her. This man, whom I decided to call Warren because it is my own brother's name and because it sounded a bit like "warm" (which this character is, warm in the sense that objects seem warmed by being near him), wanted to take his wife on a short holiday to the sea coast in order to help mend the rift which had formed between them shortly after their first child had arrived. He didn't understand why, but in the past few months his wife had retreated to a world of her own and everything he thought of to say to her sounded gauche and inappropriate and made him feel more and more of a stranger to her. At first he thought it was just that they needed more time together so he had taken a leave from work. It had not proved successful. She began to isolate herself even more. One day she had brought home a record by a singer called Patti Smith, someone he had never heard of before, and it had hurt him to realize that the days when their taste in music had been almost identical were over. Always somewhat unpredictable and emotional, she nevertheless had held certain definite values which they had shared. Now she began to talk about finding her own apartment where she could think undisturbed. As if *he* disturbed *her*.

Nancy and Warren's house backed onto a narrow river (in places it was only a stream) which bisected the city. In the very early spring the river, though still partly frozen, rushed madly, frothingly, by, past the ice bridges that were being licked up by the sun even as you watched them. And although the river had its beauty, the rest of the city at that time of year was morose and brown, the left-over snow greyly porous. It was the time of year when people waited for the mailman and snatched the letters almost from his hands. There was nothing to do; the skating rinks had long melted and the city crews were waiting for everything to dry enough to start the flower beds. I called Warren's wife Nancy because it is the name my mother almost called me.

Once Warren had made up his mind to take Nancy to the coast, he felt immediately better, and then worse. Better, because he thought that that was all they really needed to make things right again, time together without the baby, then worse, because he realized that it was such a meager attempt at a solution to a problem he sensed was very large. It became apparent to him, as they prepared to leave, that she was only going for his sake, that she didn't want to go at all.

Just before they were to leave for the airport, Warren thought that he would go down to the river behind

their house and take their dog for one last walk, giving
Nancy a chance to feed the baby in peace. He began
to throw rocks for the dog to chase. He fingered a rock,
holding it between his thumb and forefinger, jerking it
outward, once, twice, three times, to tease the dog. When
he let the rock go, the dog was off instantly into the
rushing water after it. Warren took up another and
followed it with his eyes as it slithered and skipped across
the still partially frozen river into a fresh hole that the
current had made. He wanted to go in and tell Nancy
that he had seen a new opening upstream and that it
wouldn't be long before the whole river was free. But
he knew he would not. The same river which marked
the seasons for him as nothing else could, for her was
just a grey and lonely gush framed by the window, as
arbitrary as air. She didn't know where it came from
and she didn't know where it was going.

He knew that she was looking down at him from their
upper storey window, watching the wind flap his old
brown ski jacket around his body. He knew that she was
waiting for him to return to the house (she had even
seemed vaguely angry when he left, why he did not
know), staring down at him as if he were wasting time.
He had dragged the big white suitcase up from the base-
ment for her and left it open on the bed for her packing
before he had gone out. But there must have been
something else she wanted him to do and had decided
not to mention. Warren called the dog to him and walked
to the house, not wanting to leave, but worried about
staying too long.

Nancy was in the kitchen washing off the high chair
with a blue cloth. The baby was crying on the floor, all
bundled up in his snowsuit, his face red. Warren picked

him up and pulled off his woollen hat. "Are you all set?"
he asked the baby, joggling him on one arm. "Are we
ready?" he asked Nancy. "Is the suitcase packed?"

"It's upstairs," she said. "Could you see about the
windows? I'll gather up his things." But instead of moving away from him, Nancy poked a finger into a jagged
rip in his jacket sleeve. She seemed to want to say
something, to be looking for something to say. He
thought he would put the baby down and put his arms
around her, but she patted his sleeve as if she felt sorry
for him. "I'll get his things," she said and left the
kitchen.

"Leave the suitcase," he shouted after her. "I'll get
it in a minute."

Warren set the baby in the back seat of the car and
went around the outside of the house to check all the
ground floor windows. When he returned he saw Nancy
at the door trying to heave and bump the heavy suitcase down, one stair at a time. "Really, Nancy," he
said, "what are you trying to do?" As if he would have
forgotten it, or was too slow for her. Without looking
at her, he took the suitcase from her and brought it out
to the car in the driveway. Then he left Nancy strap-
ping the baby into his car seat and went upstairs to
change his jacket.

They drove to Warren's parents', where the baby was
going to stay while they were away. When they left, Nancy kissed the baby over and over and said, "I love you,
be good." She reminded his mother to put the baby's
hat on when she took him out and that made Warren
angry. "Nancy, he doesn't need a hat, it's April." But
she told him that it wasn't quite April yet, suddenly
planting her feet on the front steps of his parents' home

as if she would have to be dragged away. On the way
to the airport, the car seat behind them seemed like the
stiff white shadow of the baby.

But he became more optimistic when the plane lifted
off. He noticed for the first time that Nancy was wearing new shoes. They had straps which crisscrossed over
her feet, making them seem vulnerable inside the crowded hulk of the plane, her painted toes like chokecherries
that would squash and spurt red if they were stepped on.

He peered out the plane window, and tried to name
the mountain peaks in his mind. If it hadn't turned out
so clear, Warren would have been disappointed. As it
was, there were enough low clouds to take the edge off
Mt. Assiniboine's distinctive horn. There were the
Selkirks, there was Mt. Sir Douglas. Warren wanted to
turn to Nancy and name them for her, to name the
mountains and the greenish lakes that hung among them,
but he knew he wouldn't try. He wanted to ask her to
remind him to buy a guidebook on the Selkirks when
they got to Vancouver, but he was afraid suddenly to
admit his need for such a concrete thing.

Warren knew that their suitcase would be the last one
down the chute at the Vancouver airport and that
somehow it would be his fault. He stood close to the
carousel, one of them had to, scrutinizing every piece
of luggage as it slid down through the flap at the top.
It reminded him of all the times he waited to be picked
up at the end of August from summer camp, when he
watched each boy wave goodbye at him so smugly from
the back seat as they were driven through the front gate.
Nancy was sauntering up and down in front of the Hertz
booth, impatient again, as if she were waiting for someone, but not him. Warren wished that he had remem-

bered how long the luggage often took to appear and
suggested that they go for a quick coffee or something.
But it was too late for that now. He saw her catch the
eye of a ground steward with a white stripe down each
pant leg. Then *he* was impatient — where was that god-
damned suitcase? There it was; it had circled once
without his noticing it. As he picked it off, he knew it
was a good thing Nancy hadn't seen it going around and
around like that or she would have rushed over and snapped it off so fast, and left him standing there like Simple Simon. When, finally, he came up behind her, he
wanted to think of something clever to whisper in her
ear. Imagine, he though, as if that would have made a
difference.

Warren decided that they would take a city bus to their
hotel down the beach road instead of the airport service.
But as soon as they had boarded, Nancy informed him
that she wanted to walk part of the way. So he began
to study the transit map above their heads, figuring it
all out, making his calculations, trying to choose the best
spot to get off.

The coastal city was marvellous in the early spring.
The trees were beginning to bloom and people were getting on the bus in sweatshirts and shorts. Every balcony
they passed seemed to have a bicycle on it. Along the
side streets outside all the greengrocers were risers loaded
with plastic buckets of fresh flowers. A girl with very long
reddish hair came down the aisle toward Warren, clutch-
ing a bunch of what looked like gardenias. He couldn't
ever recall seeing ones quite so brilliant; they were a deep
shade of pink, with an explosion of scent. He realized
that she must have been smelling them with great ab-
sorption as she waited for the bus, for the stamens had

left a mustard-coloured dusting on the underside of her nose. This sight affected him deeply; it was genuine and artless.

Then Nancy tugged at his sleeve and asked him, as a child would, "When can we get off, Warren?" He tried to warn her, "It's a long walk from here yet," but her mind was made up. She gave the cord above their heads two quick jerks, jumped down to the sidewalk before he knew it, and stood there holding the door half-open for him and the suitcase. Then she let the door bang against his legs as she dashed on up ahead of him.

The suitcase was very heavy, and though he tried to walk fast, to catch up with her, Warren could see that he wouldn't be able to. Finally he had to put it down on the sidewalk and rest his hand, and she turned around to glare at him as if she might kick her heels out at him. He flexed and unflexed his hand to get the ache out of it, and then pointed down the beach to the hotel's large sign. "Look, Nancy," he said, "there it is, just a little way, not far now."

Nancy gazed away at it, and said nothing, just waited for him, shifting in her shoes. They must have been hurting her, he thought, for they were higher heeled than she normally bought, but she would not have admitted it. He wanted to say to her, let's take our time, what's the hurry, we're on holiday, let's sit down and look at the ships a minute — *look at the ships!* — but she was breathing impatiently. He picked up the suitcase again and she surged ahead, not looking back.

After a few minutes more, Warren was forced to lean over, to support the weight of the suitcase on his leg. He could sense the muscle in his left cheek twitching from the strain and the tension. Above the swash of the waves, he was sure he could hear her short breaths of annoyance.

Then she stopped. Warren caught up with her and put the suitcase down gratefully, hoping to catch his breath for a minute, hoping she would now look with him over the sea. Was there anything in the world that represented as much freedom as a ship? Because for him the sea was endless, and the sea air full of hope. *Look at the ships!*

But Nancy grabbed the handle of the suitcase from him. Warren felt his face tighten and his eyes, unblinking, feel the cold salt air. Don't you dare, don't you dare: the words stiffened inside him. She would not take the suitcase from him, she would not. He would not allow it.

And yet Nancy took a firm hold of the handle and began to walk away with it ahead of him. It was an almost impossible burden for her, but she was carrying it. She squared her shoulders and put one foot in front of the other. It was the back of her head that he resented, the blank wall of hair. Hurrying to catch her, he dashed out his hand and wrenched the suitcase from her with such force that the sudden friction scalded his palm. Nancy put her hand on his arm and said in a voice one would use to speak to an older person, "Warren, let me take it."

He would not let her take it. He decided then that he would never let her take it if he had to stand there until he fell down. He did not move, only glared at her with no breath left, it seemed, to form words. Without thinking it, he knew that the words were inside him and that they were strong, but that if he brought them out into the open, in front of her, they would turn limp and ineffective. So he did not speak or move.

But, inexplicably, she moved. She came over to him

and rested her head on his chest. He could see the top of her head now and he liked that better. There was a straight white part down the middle, a tender seam. Warren eased the suitcase down to the sidewalk and took her head in both his hands. He cupped his fingers around her head to feel the small roundness of it. Spreading his fingers, he pressed them lightly into her head until he could feel the delicate bones of her skull, and his hands containing it.

I tried many times to go on, to finish that story but it stubbornly resisted. At times it had even seemed physically painful to add another word. I didn't like Nancy; she was unkind to her husband who loved her. And perhaps because of this I began to hate the room where I went to write and the sad building with its long dark corridors and strange name. I decided to get rid of the story. One day before I left I unscrewed a section of the radiator under the window and laid the story carefully rolled up inside. If the Soma building is torn down on Hallowe'en, 1984, then one day I will be walking by there, look up, and find it gone, as if it were never there at all, and then perhaps I will start again.

Allan's office was twice the size of mine and attached to it by a door which he kept locked and covered over on his side by a wall of particle board. I had sublet my office from him. Originally intended as a series of adjoining offices, Allan rented the two on either side of him until his model business grew large enough to take up more space. He told me that he would occupy mine when I left. Along each wall were tables on which he cut the large sheets of coloured plastic into the small squares and rectangles he needed for the walls of his tiny buildings.

The spring I was there he was working on a model for a new penitentiary that was to be built near Saskatoon.

The day I left permanently, I knocked on his door and let myself in. "I'm going now," I said. "Everything's out in the van. I wanted to tell you how much I've enjoyed knowing you."

Allan was sitting on a stool joining two tiny red walls, dipping their edges in solvent and butting the sides together. He stood the corner up on the table in front of him. The wings of the building were colour-coded, red for the staff offices. "Pull up a stool," he said.

"I don't have time," I told him. "I just wanted to say goodbye." And then I thought of something else. "Remember about the demolition date, Hallowe'en, 1984? Why do you think they picked that date? Doesn't it seem an odd date?"

"Oh, not at all," he said. "From what I've heard it is completely arbitrary. As a matter of fact, the guy downstairs told me that it probably won't be brought down on that date at all. Apparently this building was supposed to have been torn down lots of times before, and escaped. It's just a phony date." Allan picked up the corner he had just made, dipped it in the solvent again, and attached it to another one already made to form a square enclosure for the red wing. The building was going to be enormous. It had a blue gymnasium in the centre and the different coloured wings radiated out from it at the end of white hallways. It fascinated me. A building would be built exactly like Allan's model; it would consist, I realized, of a series of compartments like the tackle boxes fishermen carry. A part of me wanted to shrink whenever I saw those rooms, to lose my bulk and my resistance.

I had another question for Allan. "I looked up *soma* in my Latin dictionary," I told him, "and it means sleep. Why do you suppose they called the building that?"

Allan laughed. "It's not sleep," he said, "It's Amos. The guy who first owned the building was called Amos, so he just turned his name around."

Those pieces of information disturbed me. But I thanked him again, closed the door to Allan's office and went back to my own. I took down the last poster, something which had become so much a part of the wall, I had forgotten it. I rolled it up, locked my door, and shoved the key under Allan's door. Then I went down the long hall to the elevator and stood waiting for it to reach the sixth floor.

That my father had himself tried to write stories was something he told me on my thirtieth birthday. He phoned me long distance, and the first thing I remember telling him was that I was happy. I was so happy, I said, that I didn't know what to do with it all. Use it, he said without hesitation. He told me to use my own happiness to make others happy. Then he told me a joke.

A little later we got to talking about my writing. He told me that I was succeeding where he had failed, that each time he had written a story, he had burned it. Best thing, too, he said, they weren't worth keeping. I tried not to sound disappointed. We talked some more, about my new baby, and about the weather. He knew exactly what kind of weather I had been having because he listened to the national weather reports daily on the radio, because weather had always been crucial to him, affecting his moods and his physical comfort even though he did not go out. He said, "Get the snow shovel out, I hear you're in for a storm." And then we said goodbye.

And he was right. Even as I replaced the receiver, the first light flakes of the winter began to float down. I sat there until they coated the spruce along the river, and the brown lawn turned white. The whole, my father wrote in his notebook, cannot be understood, but it can be believed in. And: When I considered what little chance I had of saying anything truly original I was overwhelmed. And: Is the two-fold character of existence a kind of oscillating identity? And: This morning the weather is calm and mild.

Gloria Sawai

$$3 \text{ poems} = 1 \text{ story}$$
$$3 \text{ p} = 1 \text{ s}$$
$$\text{p} = \frac{\text{s}}{3}$$

1 A Poem for Jim

I have completed three rows of the afghan. The first is purple, the second blue, the third violet. I am knitting it in loose and even stitches for lightness and warmth against the winter nights. I knit only in the early evening while I wait for supper to cook. Later I'll prepare my lessons for the mathematics classes I will teach tomorrow. The waiting is brief, my supper simple. I cook only for myself. At this rate the afghan will take two months — or even three — to complete.

The phone rang in September on a windy evening at
dusk. I was sitting near the window in the leather chair,
the one I'd bought for Steve in '62. Geometric theorems
were spread before me on the floor in neat designs. In
the kitchen, the soup had just begun to simmer on a
burner turned to low. Outside, branches of the elm
scraped against the siding.

I stuck the metal needles into the ball of purple yarn,
laid the knitting on my lap, and reached to the side table
for the receiver. It would be my mother. She's a widow
too, and when she calls it's always in that near-dark-but-
not-quite time of day.

"Hello," I said, counting the last five stitches in the
row. I had ended on purl.

"M-m-m-m-m-m-m-m-m-m-m-m-m-m-m-m- ..."

"Hello?" I asked. "Whom are you calling?"

"M-m-m-m-m-m-m-m-m-m-m-m-m-m-m-m- . . ."

"Were you calling 469-2801?"

"M-m-m-m-m-m-m-m-m-m-m-m-m-m-m-m-m-m-
m-m-m-m-m-m . . ."

"I'm sorry. You must have the wrong . . ."

"MY NAME IS J-J-J-J-J-J-J-J-JIM!"

"Oh. Well, this is Carolyn Janz," I said. "Were you
calling me?" I picked up my knitting. I recounted the
last four boxes of the row.

"I-I-I-I-I-I-I-I-I-I-I'm taking a-a-a-a-a-a-a-a-a-a-a-
a-a-a SURVEY."

"Survey?"

"Foothills H-H-H-H-H-H-H-H-HOSPITAL."

"Oh."

"THERAPY!"

"I see."

"W-w-w-w-w-w-w-w-w-w-w-w-w-would you a-a-a-a-a-a-a-a-a-a-a-answer a few QUESTIONS?''

He sounded intense, nervous. His voice was loud.

''Yes,'' I said. ''I suppose I could . . . if it doesn't take too long. But if my supper starts boiling on the stove, well, you understand. So, what could I help you with?''

''D-d-d-d-d-d-d-d-d-d-d-d-do you think a-a-a-a-a-a-a-a-a-a-speech impediment is a H-H-H-H-H-H-H-H-H-H-HANDICAP?''

''Well,'' I said. ''That's an interesting question, isn't it. I hadn't thought about it much. I suppose it could be. Perhaps it depends on what one is doing, what line of work he's in. If one were in some kind of public relations, politics or such, then I would think . . . yes, I do believe that a speech impediment in that case would be a handicap. But if one were to choose a different line of work — in a library perhaps. Or a mine. A coal mine, or some such place as that, then it may not be such a handicap. Actually it's hard to say, isn't it? I don't really know. What do you think about that? Do you think a speech impediment is a handicap?

My right leg had begun to ache. I twisted my body in the leather chair to let my weight rest on my left thigh. The ball of yarn fell to the floor. The silver needle dangled from the purple bundle.

''I-I-I-I-I-I-I-I think a-a-a-a-a-a-a-a- speech impediment is a ha-a-a-a-a-a-a-a-a-a-a-andicap.''

His voice was quiet.

''Yes, I guess you're right. I guess I would have to agree with you there.''

He asked two more questions, then he thanked me, most sincerely he said, and I hung up the receiver. I picked up the yarn from the floor, removed the silver needles, and counted the stitches.

Knitting is like mathematics, and like poetry. All three are concerned with making patterns. Occasionally I dabble in poetry, no doubt for this very reason. Recently I have begun a new poem. I have written the first line: Purple is the colour of irises.

2 A Poem for Joe

I'm nervous when the phone rings in the night. Maybe someone is ill. Or perhaps dead.

In October it rang. I threw off the quilt and sat up, my heart pounding. I slid off the bed, felt my way through the silent room, across the corridor, and into the living room. I fumbled with the receiver, lifted it from its black nest on the end table.

"Yes?" I said. "This is Carolyn Janz."

His voice was dark, oval as a cave, and distantly familiar. "Guess whooooo?"

I sat down in the leather chair, the leather cold and stiff against the thin fabric of my night dress, against my back under the fabric, and my bare arms leaning. "I don't know," I said. I snapped on the floor lamp, swivelled my chair around to see the clock on the wall by the door. 2 a.m.

"Guess whooo?" he said again. The voice was blue-black, lit only by echoes, glasses tinkling in some far-off smokey room.

"I really don't want to guess. If you won't tell me, I'll just . . ."

"It's your old buddy." The voice lightened, took on a shape, something I'd seen before, in a room somewhere, or street. In a corridor, or perhaps a cab.

"Your voice sounds familiar, but I can't place you. I honestly can't. Why don't you tell me?"

"You don't remember, huh? You've forgot your good old buddy."

"If you won't tell me, I . . ."

"Think. Row six, seat four, by the window."

So that's who it was, an old student of mine from a math class sometime in the vague past. But I have been a teacher of mathematics for fifteen years now. At 150 students a year, the total is well over 2,000. And he wanted me to remember him in row six, seat four, by the window. It was absurd.

And then I did. I saw him sitting there in the fourth seat near the window, his wide shoulders hunched over the desk top, his black hair hanging sharp and heavy to his shoulders, his smooth brown face, the delicate scar from his lip to his ear.

"Well, for heaven's sake. Holy Whiteman. How are you?"

"I am fine — and — dandy. Long — time — no — see. Ha."

"Not so long," I said. "Only a year in fact. When did you get out?"

"I was *re*—leased exactly four days ago, on October the fifth, at exactly nine minutes and thirty-seven seconds past twelve o'clock noon."

"And what have you been doing since then?"

"What have I been doing? Ha."

"I guess it's good to be out," I said. "Are you living in town?"

"I am presently *re*—siding at the Royal George Hotel. Room 200. High class."

I laughed.

"Let me tell you about it," he said. "Number one: windows — with curtains. Number two — bedspread — pink — ha. Number three — mirror. Number four: toilet — with lid."

"It sounds classy," I said.

"You wanna see it?" he asked. "You wanna come over? I'll make you a cup of coffee. Instant Maxwell House."

"It sounds inviting," I said.

"Ha."

I leaned forward in the leather chair, the leather warmer now and more pliable, my back lingering for a moment against the leather.

"It was nice talking to you, Joe, but I'm still a math teacher you know. I have to get my sleep."

"Hey. Why didn't you answer my letters?"

The question came too abruptly for me to formulate a decent reason.

"I'm not very good at letters," I said. "But I did answer one of them, remember? You got the one I sent last Christmas with the list."

"I got the list all right. Some list."

"Don't complain," I said. "You got a pen pal out of it, didn't you?"

"Out of fourteen females on that there list, one female answers my letter — your mother."

"I guess people just don't like writing letters," I said. I leaned back in the leather chair, the leather warm and moist against my arms.

"Your mother must be getting pretty old," he said.

"She's over seventy. Why?"

"She says funny things."

"Like what?"

"Like — trust God, everything will turn out."

"That's how she is," I said. "She talks like that."

"She has funny writing," he said. "I couldn't hardly read her writing."

"I know. It's a scrawl. Well, Joe, I . . ."

"Hey. Do you wanna know what I'm gonna do some day? Some day I'm gonna buy me a ticket on the Greyhound Bus, and I'm gonna hop on that bus, and I'm gonna go and visit your mother."

"Wouldn't she be pleased," I said.

Picture my mother in Lakeside Apartments, number 203. In quilted robe she sinks back in the soft cushions of her floral sofa. She gazes out the large and spotless window framed with drapery, beige to match the rug. She's looking out on Mirror Lake, the water smooth, the grass at its edge, clipped and tidy. The door bell rings. She rises from her chair, walks carefully across the room, her footsteps neatly impressed in the rug's deep pile.

Picture Joe Holy Whiteman. Six foot three, blue black hair, swarthy skin, and scar from lip to ear. He stands on the red carpet of the foyer, under the chandelier, smiling, eager to meet my mother, maybe to ask, "What do you mean — trust God and everything will turn out?"

Picture Mrs. Williams across the hall, who keeps track of things. Who orders her groceries on Friday, has her rooms cleaned by Olga Storch on Saturday, travels by Yellow Cab to the United Church on Sunday morning, writes to her daughter Eunice, married to a realtor in Toronto (and he's doing so well, she says) on Sunday afternoon, and sips tea as she watches television on Sunday evening.

Picture all the residents of Lakeside Apartments. And

Joe Holy Whiteman standing on the red carpet under the chandelier.

"You must do that some time," I said. "But listen, Joe, I really have to get some sleep . . ."

"Yea. You better get back to your old man. He must be getting cold, alone there all by himself. Ha."

"Do you mean my husband?"

"That's what I said."

"My husband isn't living."

"You mean he's . . ."

"He's dead."

"Oh. I'm sorry to hear that. How did it happen?" He spoke softly. His voice was gentle.

"He was killed in a car accident near Red Deer."

"No. When was this?"

"Let's see. It must be nine years ago now."

"Oh. I'm sorry. That's too bad."

"Thanks," I said. "It's all right."

"You're what they call a widow then, is that it?"

"I guess that's what they call it." I swivelled the chair around to look at the clock by the door. It was 2:15. I stood up, stretched, yawned, dug my toes into the green pile of the carpet. "Really, Joe, I . . ."

"Hey. What about the kids? How did your kids take that?"

"I don't have any children," I said.

"No kids?"

"No."

"Really? No kids?"

"That's right."

"I'm sorry," he said. "That's too bad."

"Why?" I asked.

"Why! Woman was made for kids."

"Women are free now. Haven't you heard?"

"Woman was made for kids."

"Some women. Not me." I sat back, stretched my legs out, then raised them and curled them against me in the leather chair. I was wide awake now. Sleep was out of the question.

"Hey. Would you do what they call in school a experiment? A scientific experiment?"

"Sure. Why not."

"But don't take it as no disrespect. You're a very respectable woman. And I don't mean no disrespect."

"What is it?"

"Do you know that big mirror they got in the window at the Hudson Bay Company?"

"Yes."

"Well, you're standing on the sidewalk by Hudson Bay in front of that there mirror. Right?"

"Right."

"And you do not have a stitch of clothes on, see? And you're looking in that mirror. Now, you start from the top of your head. You look at the top of your head, then you go down. Down, down, down, till you get to your feet. But before you get to your feet, you stop at each part and you ask yourself a question — 'What is that there part for?' You got that? For each part you say, 'what is that there part for?' "

"Got it."

"All right. Get ready. Get set. Go. And don't forget the belly button. Ha."

"Okay," I said. "Here I go. Down . . . down . . . down . . ."

"Where are you now?"

"My knees."

"Ohh. Your eyes travel very fast."

"There, I'm finished. I'm on my big toe."

"See? It proves." He sounded triumphant.

"Proves what?" I asked.

"Woman was made for kids."

I laughed.

"Hey. Do you wanna cup of coffee? Instant Maxwell House?"

"I'm afraid not."

"I don't mean right now. Later sometime?"

"Well, I'm pretty busy . . . "

"You are a verry respectable woman. I guess you don't want no coffee."

"Mostly I'm just a busy woman," I explained. "My days are full."

"I guess you don't want no coffee with a ex-con, huh? With a ex-con Indian?"

"Joe . . ."

"You wouldn't wanna be with no God damn Indian, huh? You wouldn't fuck no Indian."

The receiver was moist in my hand. It slipped. I caught it and held it for a moment beneath my chin and against my chest. And I wondered for an instant if he were on the other end of the line, listening. And could he hear it? Did he hear it there under the thin cloth, hardly covering? I raised the receiver to my ear, pressed it hard against my ear.

"Ohh," he said, so softly that I strained to listen. "I am very sorry."

Recently I have been studying the mathematical concept of function. I have been thinking about something I read in a book once. I have been thinking about this:

If the proposition "y is a function of x" means that all the possible values of the first term are determined by all the possible values of the second, then it is upon this fact, rather than upon the value of x as such that y depends. In the end, therefore, the true determinant is the character of the relationship that unites the two terms. And so the formula, $y = F(x)$, is seen to be a superficial rendering of the formula, $y = F(xy)$

I have completed six rows of the afghan. I'm getting nowhere with poetry. Purple is the colour of irises . . .

3 A Poem for Mother

In November my mother calls. It's five o'clock, the usual time. She says the usual things.

"I thought I'd call. I haven't heard from you and I wonder about you. I wonder how you're doing, but I don't hear."

Then I say the usual things: I've been busy, my health is good, and the weather is fine. I repeat the words several times.

She tells me the weather in Winnipeg is cold — 30 degrees below zero fahrenheit; and I should be thankful I live in Alberta, where there are warm chinooks. She tells me that Aunt Mary is in the Bethany Home now because she can't manage anymore living by herself, and why don't I send my aunt a letter, or at least a card.

Then she asks, "Whatever happened to that nice young Indian fellow who used to write to me? I haven't heard from him for quite awhile. He seemed like such a pleasant young man."

"He's out now," I tell her. "He's out of jail."

"Did you hear me?" she says. "I asked you what happened to that Indian. You remember, the one who wrote to me?"

"He's OUT," I holler into the receiver.

"Out? You mean out of jail?"

"YES."

"Well, now, isn't that nice. I'm happy to hear that. I'm very pleased to hear that. Have you heard how he's doing? Is he working? Do you think he'll straighten out?"

I try to explain. "It's kind of hard you know. They just put you on a Greyhound Bus with a few dollars in your pocket, and send you into the city — with no place to go and nothing in particular to do."

"There must be something wrong with this line again," she says. "I think it's the cold weather. I asked you about that Indian. Has he got a job? Is he working? Do you think he'll straighten out?"

"I was just saying it's hard. They put you on a Greyhound Bus with . . ."

"Just a minute," she says. "There's a wire on this hearing aid that sometimes gets disconnected."

I sit back in the leather chair, twisting my body into a more comfortable position, wishing that I'd called her yesterday when I thought about it.

"I was asking you about that Indian," she says loudly. "Do you think he'll straighten out?"

"YES!" I shout into the receiver.

"Well, I'm happy to hear that. I'm so pleased. Isn't that just fine."

She reminds me again that Aunt Mary is in the Bethany Home because she can't live alone anymore. And wouldn't she enjoy a letter from me, or even a postcard. Then I tell her that I'll write soon, and to Aunt Mary too, and I hang up.

I am on the ninth row of the afghan. I had thought to have it finished by winter, January at the latest. Now I think it won't be done until spring, or even summer. It lies in a purple heap in a wicker basket beside the leather chair.

Nor have I finished the poem I started. I can't seem to get past the third line:

Purple is the colour of irises,
of bruises,
and of kings' robes.

Maybe the other lines will come later. Perhaps in the dark of a winter night a pattern will emerge, an appropriate closure. If not, does it matter? I'm a Sunday poet.

It is mathematics that will ultimately sustain me. I concur with Alfred North Whitehead, who said that mathematics is more nearly precise, comes closer to the truth. In a thousand years, he said, it may be as common a language as speech is today. At any rate, I am more confident here, with the clear, inevitable patterns of mathematics: patterns to build roads and bridges by, powerful intricate patterns to hurl rockets into space, to send them even past the moon, speeding through vast black silences toward unknown planets.

Brenda Riches

SNOW FLURRIES

The black and white cat sits beside the porcelain lamp and washes herself. Lamplight patches her body with silver. It was the sound of her tongue that woke me: the lapping of water trickling from a broken gutter. Now she stretches her hind leg forward and rasps her tongue from the thigh to the thick white of her paw. Her whiskers flatten against her face as she bends to clean herself, then spring out again when she lifts her head to look at me.

Last year she was a kitten. She lay on my child's lap, her white paw a plumed fan held over a delicate nose, her eyes thin lines. The child's hand lay slack on soft black fur, the fingers slightly curled. Nothing moved on her closed face, but her chest moved, her breaths gently in tune with the kitten's rough purr.

Safe in their breathing, I sat and watched them till they woke up.

* * *

The rink is a busy blur of children. They are birds, wings stretched, making patterns on the cloudy ice. I watch from a wooden bench whose red paint is scratched so that the old black shows through.

One little girl wears a skirt of flamingo pink that flutters against her jaunty buttocks as she jerks across the ice, a thick white sweater, its sleeves tucked into snowy gloves, white tights snug on her legs. She is flamboyant and warm, a bright fledgeling with her fluffy hair and struggling arms. Eyes lit with hunger: for spins and jumps, for spectators in darkness, for the spotlight sun to shine on her golden flight.

My child is at the far side, practising the same movement again and again. In her dark dress she looks so thin, her limbs like twigs.

This evening, before we came, I called to her. "Come and look at the sunset." She sighed, looked briefly at the engorged sky, then went back to her room. I sat in the rocker and waited out the light, the evening. All that brightness was slowly sucked down by the horizon, and littered clouds were left to disintegrate into darkness. I rubbed my hands over the worn plush of the chair's arms. My fingers lingered over its harsher spots.

"It's time for my skating lesson." She snapped on the light and stood by the front door, new skates slung over one shoulder, dangling at the ends of their laces. Faded freckles smudged her white face. "Come on." She rubbed at the doorknob with a mittened hand. A

strand of brown hair fell over her face. She made no
gesture to brush it back. We walked out to the car.

I have an important job. I drive my child to the place
she wants to be, where she moves in a geometry of her
own, leaving her marks on the rink's cold floor.

I look at her distant face. She notices and looks away.

A boy in black spins effortlessly in the middle of the
rink. He starts with his hands above his head. As he
spins, he brings them spiralling down. The child is watching him too.

The siren. Time's up.

Outside, it's snowing. Sudden and thick, flakes gather
on the windshield, are pushed by the wiper blades to
become matted ice. My car eases forward through snow
that falls like pieces of plaster: flakes from some huge
ceiling.

She walks into the house, drops skates and mitts onto
the floor, pulls the white wool cap from her head. Her
hair bristles like copper wires.

"Do you want a snack?" I ask her.

"No thanks. I don't want anything." Her voice is
blunt metal. Already she's the other side of her door.

* * *

The wind is blowing the snow so high it's like a blizzard in a paperweight. I can see branches vaguely bending. Houses are hardly there. What country has my child
vanished into?

Oh the times and times I have watched her walk from
this house, along the park's beaten path, to disappear:
behind the hill, into mists, through curtains of rain or

snow. Always she walks out of sight while I stand at the window watching.

"Put on your snowsuit," I told her this morning. "And pull your toque all the way down. It's nasty out."

The cat's complaint has to struggle through two doors to reach me. When I put her out earlier, she bounded over the fence and sat on the neighbour's front porch. She must be hungry now; she's rubbing her wet body against my leg and I have to pick her up before I can close the door. She squirms and jumps down.

Lap lap. In the kitchen's quiet the cat drinks. Tiny beads of milk catch on the fur around her mouth. Now she jumps onto the stool and begins to lick at the milky fur. I pick up a cloth and wipe her wet paw marks from the linoleum with the child's old flannel nighty. It used to be white with a design of blue rabbits. Now it's grimy with dust.

She was wearing it that night she walked in her sleep, came whimpering into my room, her eyes wide open. Flecks of saliva shone at the corners of her mouth. She stood by my bed, frowning.

"What's the matter?"

"I don't know."

"Are you awake?"

"I don't know." Her eyes didn't shift, stared at the bright lampshade. The blue rabbits quivered around her slight body. I picked her up and carried her to her bed.

Today her room is a clutter of everything she won't throw out: chipped porcelain animals, a skater doll with one leg missing, an empty candy tin with an eagle totem on the lid, unfinished scraps of embroidery, last year's calendar.

She's hung the cat's photo on the wall above her bed. Caught in mid-yawn. "Did you know your cat's got a broken tooth?" the neighbour asked when he brought the photo round and gave it to her.

*   *   *

I can't see a thing; frost is too thick inside the car window. The street light beats on the outside, turning this glass into the thin white wall of a sunken candle.

Where's that child? Hanging around the concession, I'll bet, buying herself something to suck on. Or else the lesson's gone into overtime. And I have to sit in a cold car and watch my breath freeze onto the windows, because I'm too tired to go in and fetch her.

She'll want to scrape it clean. She likes to. But first she'll be scornful. She'll sigh and say the car is useless. Nothing works in it. She'll grumble as she pulls off her mitts, mutter as she jabs the scraper up and down, and then lamplight will splash into her face.

"Hi." She slides into the back seat, quiet as wax.

"What kept you so long?" I ask.

"Can't see a thing," she complains. "Where's the scraper? Jeez, it's cold."

Her face is framed in the mirror: mouth a tight line, eyes looking out onto the street, not at the working of her restless hands.

"When are we going to get a new car?" she asks.

"When When is the goose with the golden eggs, that's when."

"You could go out to work. Why don't you?"

She doesn't want an answer. She's muttering little clouds of breath onto the window. "Could at least get this shitty tit of a heater working right." Then she leans back, her mouth pinched into a smile, and waits to be told off.

"You're right," I say. "It's a shit of a heater."

* * *

The rattan horse lies on its side, face cushioned on a rise of snow. I suppose that's my fault; I told her to throw it out. But look at it now, under the cold moon. Stray pieces of straw binding lie curled on the snow. One ear has broken off completely and lies a few inches from the head.

"Throw it out," I'd said. "It's no good any more."

"We could get it mended." Her face turned pink.

"No point. You never ride it anyway."

"I do *so* ride it." Flints in her voice.

"Not that *I* ever see."

"The trouble with *you*, Mother, is that you never want to mend *anything*."

* * *

"Which movement did you do wrong?"

"The left right left right Mohawk." Her face is slippery with tears.

"It doesn't matter." Stupid thing to say. "You can take the test again, can't you?"

"I did it the way they taught me." The words jerk out between sobs. "They taught me wrong." Her lower lip is crimson where her teeth have bitten into it. "It's not fair." Her sobs build and topple over. I brush the sticky hair from her face.

"I'll speak to the instructor if you like."

"Don't bother. I don't want to go skating ever again. It's goodamn piss-awful BORING."

* * *

She's wearing her new nighty. False patchwork. Her face is the colour of watery milk, her eyes rimmed with the charcoal of fatigue.

"Go back to bed."

"Why don't you?"

"I don't feel sleepy," I tell her honestly.

"Me neither." Her eyelids tell me she's lying.

She won't sleep, knowing that I'm sitting by myself at this table. She stands in the doorway, shifting her weight from one foot to the other, while the cat butts her legs.

* * *

A boy is flying his kite out there in all that cold. A black plastic kite, gliding like a raven. The boy has to run to keep the string taut. He runs easily over the ridges of frozen snow, his face tilted to watch the flight of his shiny bird.

I stand still, tap turned off, bubbles weakening in the sink, and feel a pulse thrum behind my forehead. Water spirals into the drain, leaving scummy pieces of grease and pallid cabbage shreds clinging to the dull chrome.

My child is walking the beaten path from the hill, swinging her skates as she comes home. Does she notice the boy there, watching her? Does she see his dark bird caught between two ridges of snow?

She picks her way over the stiff ground, stamping her feet down hard in the crumbly parts so that a sharp spray flies up, She flings the door open.

"Hi, Mom."

Against my hot cheek her face is alive with cold.

Bonnie Burnard

CRUSH

It's Thursday morning and it's hot, hot, hot. The girl is painting the kitchen cupboards. The paint stinks up the kitchen, stinks up the whole house. Her summer blonde pony tail and her young brown shoulders are hidden in the cupboards and a stranger coming into the kitchen, seeing only the rounded buttocks in the terrycloth shorts and the long well formed legs, might think he was looking at part of a woman.

She's tired. She babysat last night. It isn't the best job she can get; there are other kids, easier kids. She takes the job because of him, because she loves to ride alone with him on the way home. He is Allen, the breadman; she thinks she loves him. She remembers him at the beach, throwing his kids around in the water, teaching them to swim. His back and thighs she will

remember when she is seventy and has forgotten others.
She does not try to imagine anything other than what
she has seen. It is already more than enough.

Her mother stands over the ironing board just inside
the dining room door. Thunk, hiss, thunk, hiss. The kitchen table separates them. It is piled high with dishes
and tea towels and bags of sugar and flour and pickling
salt. Jars of spices are pitched here and there, rest askew
in the crevices of the pile. The cupboards are hot and
empty. She has nearly finished painting the inside of
them.

Neither the girl nor her mother has spoken for over
an hour. It is too hot. She leans back out of the cupboards, unbuttons her blouse and takes it off, tossing
it to the table. It floats down over the dishes. She wants
to take off her bra, but doesn't.

"You be careful Allen doesn't catch you in that state
young lady. He'll be along with the bread soon." Her
mother doesn't lift her head from the ironing. Her
sleeveless housedress is stained with sweat. It soaks down
toward her thick waist.

Maybe I want him to, the girl thinks. She does not
share this thought with her mother. Her mother doesn't
know about backs and thighs.

"Have you picked out the bathing suit you want?"
Her mother glances up at her. The bathing suit is to be
the reward for the painting. "It's time you started thinking about modesty. It's beginning to matter."

"No." The girl drags the fresh blue paint over the
old pale green. But she has picked out her suit. It's the
one on the dummy in the window downtown, the one
the boys stare at. She knows she won't be allowed to have
it. Mrs. Stewart in the ladies shop wouldn't even let her

try it on. Said it wasn't suitable for her. But it does suit
her. She wants it.

She hears the scream of the ironing board as her
mother folds it up and again her mother's voice.

"I'm going downtown for meat. You put that blouse
on before I leave."

"Why?" The girls looks at the limp skin on her
mother's arm. "Nobody's here."

"Because Allen's coming with the bread soon, that's
why. Now get it on. I'm as hot as you are and you don't
see me throwing my clothes off."

Her mother stands checking the money in her purse,
waiting til the last button is secure before she heads for
the back door. "I'll bring you some cold pop." The
screen door slams.

The girl steps down from the paint-splattered chair,
goes to the sink, turns on the water and lets it run cold.
She opens the freezer door, takes out a tray of ice cubes.
She fills a glass with ice, slows the tap, watches the water
lap around the ice cubes as it seeks the top of the glass.
She drinks slowly. She isn't thirsty, but it's the only way
to get something cold inside her. She pulls an ice cube
out of the glass, holds it in her hands, feels it begin to
melt against the heat of her palm. She raises her hand
to her forehead, rubs the ice against her skin, back into
her hair, over her neck, down into the sweaty shadow
between her breasts. The ice cube is small now, just a
round lump. Her hand is wet.

When he danced with her at the Fireman's dance, his
hand was wet. Not the same wet though, not the same
at all. His buddies hollered things about him liking the
young stuff and they all laughed, even the wives. She
laughed too, pretended she understood how funny it was,

his touching her. But the skin on her back can still feel the pressure of his arm, how it moved her the way he wanted her to move. It should have been hard to move together. But it was easy, like a dream.

She wonders how close he is to their house. She dries her hand on the tea towel hanging from the stove door. She undoes the top button of her blouse then the next and the next and the next. It falls from her hand in a heap on the floor. She unfastens her bra, slips it down over her brown arms, lets it drop on top of the blouse.

She climbs up on the chair, begins to paint again. She can't smell the paint anymore or feel the ache in her arm that the movement brings.

Turning, she sees him standing there in the kitchen with her, the basket of baking slung round his neck. She comes down from the chair, steps over the blouse and bra, stands in front of him, as still as the surface of a hot summer lake. There is no sound but the catch of his breathing, no movement but the startled rhythm of his eyes moving from her face to her warm bare skin and back again.

"Jesus," he says.

"I wanted to show you, that's all."

He goes out the door quickly, doesn't leave Thursday's two loaves of white and one whole wheat.

Her mother's voice at the door hits the girl like an iceberg. She stands frozen, knowing that she will be caught and that she will be punished. Punished in some new way. She bends down, picks up her bra.

He's in the truck and he's wishing he had farther to go than the next block. Jesus. Bread to deliver. After that. What the hell was she trying to do.

He checks the rearview mirror. Maybe her mother thinks he was in on it; she could come roaring out after him any minute. He's a sitting duck in this damned truck. A drive. He'll go for a drive, just to clear his head. Christ.

He drives out past the gas station, past the local In and Out store, out of the town, onto a grid road. He goes a few miles, lets the hot breeze blow the sweat away. He pulls over.

His wife. What if it gets back to her? She'll find some way to blame him. He should go right now and tell her the truth. Shit. She wouldn't believe him. He doesn't believe it and he was there. He'll just lie low and hope, pray, that her mother is too embarrassed to tell anyone.

The mother. What if she does think he was in on it? Maybe he should go back there right now, tell her straight out. She could watch his hands shake. No. If it's going to come up it'll come up soon and he'll just say it was a surprise and he won't be lying.

The girl has never given him one small clue that she was thinking in those terms. She's a good kid. He enjoys talking to her and he always makes a point of being nice to her when he picks her up to sit and when he drives her home. She always hides herself behind a huge pile of books held up tight to her sweater. And she helped him teach the kids to swim 'cause his wife wouldn't and he didn't even look at her, can't even picture her in a bathing suit.

So damned hot. He leans back in his seat, unbuttons his shirt, lights a cigarette. The sight of her comes back through the smoke that hangs around him. Not centrefold stuff, not even as nice as his wife before the kids but nice just the same, yeah, nice. It's been a long time since he's seen fresh, smooth, hard ones. He shifts around in his seat. Damn.

It's like she just discovered she had them. Or maybe she just got tired of being the only one who knew. Now he knows. And what's he supposed to do about it? Jesus. What she said made it sound like it was supposed to be some kind of gift. Man, this is too complicated for a Thursday morning.

The picture comes back again and this time he holds it and looks it over a little more carefully. He's sure they've never been touched. He thinks about dancing with her that once and how easy she was in his arms. Not sexy, just easy. Like she trusted him. He can't remember ever feeling that before. They sure didn't trust him when he was seventeen, had no business trusting him. And what he gets from his wife isn't trust, not exactly.

Kids are sometimes just crazy. She's crazy. But he remembers her eyes and whatever it was they were saying, it had nothing to do with being crazy.

Back the picture comes again and Jesus it is like a gift. He closes his eyes and the breasts stay in his eyes and he thinks he sees his own hands going to them and he feels a gentleness come into his hands and he sits up straight and he starts the truck and he tells himself you're crazy, man, that's who's crazy.

The mother stands watching the girl do up the last of the buttons on her blouse. She holds the package of meat in one hand, the bottle of pop in the other. The paper around the meat is dark and soft where blood has seeped out. She walks over to the fridge, puts the meat in the meat keeper and the pop beside the quarts of milk on the top shelf. She closes the fridge door with the same care she would use on the bedroom door of a sleeping child. When she turns the girl has climbed up on the chair in front of the cupbards and is lifting the brush.

"Get down from that chair," she says.

The girl puts the brush across the top of the paint can and steps down.

"I could slap you," the mother says, calmly. This is not a conversation she has prepared herself for. This is not a conversation she ever expected to have. She cannot stop herself from looking at the girl's body, cannot stop the memory of her own body and the sudden remorse she feels knowing it will never come back to her. She longs for the sting of a slap, longs to feel it on her own hand and to imagine it on the girl's cheek. But she puts the anger someplace, out of the way. She pulls a chair from the table, away from the mess of cupboard things piled there and sits in the middle of the room, unprotected.

"Sit down," she says.

The girl sits where she is, on the floor, her brown legs tucked under her young bum as they were tucked through all those years of stories, fairy tales. But the mother can smell her fear.

"How much did you take off?"

The girl does not answer. She looks directly into her mother's eyes and she does not answer.

The mother begins the only way she knows how.

"I had a crush on your father. That's how it started with us, because I had a crush on him. He was only a little older than me but I think it's the same. I don't know why it should happen with you so young but I think it's the same. The difference is I didn't take my clothes off

121

for him. And he wasn't married. It's wrong to feel that way about someone if he's married and it's wrong to take your clothes off. Do you understand?''

The girl picks at a scab on her ankle.

''The way you feel has got nothing to do with the way things are. You've embarrassed him. I could tell at the gate he was embarrassed. You won't be babysitting for them anymore. He'll tell his wife and they'll laugh about it. You've made a fool of yourself.''

The girl lifts the scab away from her skin. The mother wants to gather her in her arms and carry her up to bed.

''You will feel this way from now on. Off and on, from now on. You have to learn to live with it. I wish it hadn't happened so soon. Now you just have to live with it longer. Do you understand?''

The girl shakes her head no.

''Women have this feeling so they will marry, so they will have children. It's like a system. And you've got to live within the system. There will be a young man for you, it won't be long. Maybe five years. That's all. You've got to learn to control this thing, this feeling, until that young man is there for you.''

The mother gets up from her chair and goes to the fridge. She takes the pop out and opens it, divides it between two glasses. She hands one to the girl.

''If you don't control it you will waste it, bit by bit, and there will be nothing left. There will be no young man, not to marry. And they'll take it from you, all of them, any of them, because they can't stop themselves from taking it. It's not their responsibility. It's your responsibility not to offer it. You just have to wait, wait for the one young man and you be careful who he is, you think about it for a long time and then you marry him and then you offer it.''

The girl gets up from the floor and puts her glass on the counter by the sink.

''Can I go now?'' she asks.

The mother feels barren. She is not a mother anymore, not in the same way. It is as if the girl's undressing has wiped them both off the face of the earth.

The girl has run away from the house, out past the gas station and the beer store onto the grid road that divides the corn fields. She is sitting in a ditch, hidden, surrounded by long grass and thistles.

She likely has ruined it, likely will never babysit for them again. Not because he was embarrassed. He wasn't embarrassed, he was afraid. It's the first time she's ever made anyone afraid. She will find a way to tell him that she didn't mean to make him afraid.

She wishes her mother had slapped her. She didn't like hearing about how her mother felt about her father, it was awful, and all that talk about controlling it and getting married someday, she knows all of that. That's what everybody does and it's likely what she'll do because there doesn't seem to be any way to do anything else. Except maybe once in a while. If she learns not to get caught. And not to scare anyone.

She feels really alone and she likes it. She thinks about his back and his thighs and she thinks about standing there in front of him. It's the best feeling she's ever had. She won't give it up. She'll just be more careful. She crosses her arms in front of her, puts one hand over each small breast and she knows she isn't wrong about this feeling. It is something she will trust. She leans back into the grass, throws her arms up over her head and stares, for as long as she can, at the hot July sun.

Edna Alford

COMPANIONSHIP

There were snowflakes intact on Arla's coat. They were large and intricate and symmetrical, like the ones you see in winter illustrations of children's storybooks or on Christmas cards.

She found it hard to believe that a week had already passed since Christmas. Every year she looked forward to Christmas and Easter and summer and always she found herself melancholy afterward, had trouble believing they had come and gone, slipped into her uneventful past with everything else.

Well, to be fair, this year hadn't been altogether uneventful. After all, David had given her a diamond just before Christmas. She removed the glove from her left hand and spread her fingers, held the stone to the light. Full of fire, the salesman at People's Credit

Jewellers had said, "Take a look at this one — it's full of fire." He had gone to the window, beckoned to David and Arla to follow him. Then he held the gold ring between his index finger and thumb, up to the light.

He had been right — the stone alarmed Arla, glittered and flashed stellate patterns like fractured glass on the smooth white plaster of the wall behind the counter near the window. So they had bought it. At first Arla had been afraid to wear the ring, afraid she might lose it, forget it behind the faucets of a sink in some gas station between Calgary and Saskatoon on her way home for Christmas to show it to her folks. But all of that seemed faraway this morning and although the ring still glittered in the artificial lights still on in the lodge, and because it was still dark outside, the diamond made her sad, was cold as ice, had lost its fire.

She opened the closet door, shook the last of the melting snowflakes from her cloth overcoat and hung it up. She pulled her duty shoes out of a paper bag, put them on and tied the grey laces. They were frayed. She knew she should replace them but lately she had been forgetting to throw in a couple of extra pairs of laces when she was at Safeway's. Actually, now that she stopped to think about it, it was the same with the hose. She found herself more than once twisting and stretching them every which way to hide the runs, which were more difficult to conceal in the white hose than in the flesh-coloured tones. She put her snowboots in a corner of the closet and shut the door. She was checking the bathlist taped to the wall in the dietary kitchen when Matron Benstone walked in.

"Mrs. Dawson had a bad night," she said. "If you need any extra help today, we'll be in the office with

Miss Piedmont. The auditors are coming in today.'' She
turned and walked down the hall toward the office.

Arla went to the drawer and lifted out the communica-
tion book. She read the notation. ''Mrs. Dawson fell on
her way to the bathroom last night,'' it said. ''She has
several cuts and abrasions on her face and forehead. I
bandaged them but she never went back to sleep. Her
speech is slurred and rambling. Slight nosebleed.''

Arla felt an increasing uneasiness as she closed the
book and began to prepare the medications for breakfast.
It had already reached the stage of lying in a doughy
lump on the floor of her stomach. It was not a new sensation for Arla. After all, she had worked with the aged
for several years now and they, like time, slipped away
quickly, often without warning, leaving only white
painted hairpins and limp doilies and stained unmade
beds behind them. One day Arla noticed that a particular
lady seemed more tired than usual; the next, she was
no longer there.

Reluctantly, Arla had begun to trust her feelings,
register them like important letters or mining claims.
She'd had enough practice at Pine Mountain. She should
have learned by now. But today, and with Mrs. Dawson
at the centre of the circles of dread, she couldn't bring
herself to believe them.

Yesterday afternoon they had stood together at the
door of the lounge, Mrs. Dawson's face bright and flushed like a small girl's, her head full of plans for the party.
The party was her own. Next week she would be a hundred years old. Arla was proud of her — felt somehow
a part of her extended lifespan, and had recently spent
a fair amount of time with her making arrangements for
the celebration which was to be held at Pine Mountain.

Arla hoped there would be a write-up in the Family Life section of the *Herald,* and a picture. In any event, she would bring her own camera.

There would be a big crowd, Mrs. Dawson had told her — children and grandchildren and great-grand-children and even one great-great-grandchild, a baby, a girl. "All of these chairs," she had pursed her lips and whispered in a voice laced and deepened through ninety-nine years of usage, "will be moved back to the walls along there." She moved her bone-fragile finger in a circular motion around the room, "and there, and there. My Isabel will be bringing the food in — turkey and pies, butter tarts and dills and pickled pigs feet. None of those instant potatoes or mushed up carrots such as we have here. *Real* carrots and beet pickles and matrimonial cake. All that's to be set up by Izzy, my girl. Over there in the corner beside the piano is where the eats will be I figure. So there'll be lots of space in the centre here for the dancing."

The thought of the dancing made her crinkle her face into a smile. The face reminded Arla of an old apple. Her eyes were brilliant, lit like long-forgotten lamps which had been stored ages ago in some dark closet of one of her distant relatives.

She set her cane horizontally across the arms of a chair near the door, extended one of her withered hands toward Arla. Arla took the hand and Mrs. Dawson placed her left hand firmly on Arla's shoulder. Mrs. Dawson was very short and stooped and had to reach a difficult distance.

Without speaking, they had begun to wheel around the room in a strange, but in its own way, graceful,

shuffle-rhythmed waltz, silent except for the barely audi-
ble singing of Mrs. Dawson.

"I was waltzin' with my darlin' —" It was the Tennessee Waltz. Arla recognized it from the country dances
of her own childhood.

At the time, the whole thing had seemed sort of silly
to Arla, except that she couldn't say no to the old woman,
as if they really were in Tennessee and she had her name
printed carefully with indelible ink on the old lady's
dance card. Not that Mrs. Dawson knew what a dance
card was — would have considered them ridiculous and
superfluous and pretentious if she had known. Lord
knows there was no need for such a thing at an old-time
dance where everyone danced with everyone else, the
old with the young, the brothers with sisters, aunts with
nephews, and, Arla remembered, the women with the
women. It all depended on how you felt at the time and
what the music was.

They danced through the space between the sofas and
chairs, past the piano, its lid spectacular with four opulent
bouquets of flowers in pale grey cardboard vases. And
Arla was reminded again by the sick sweet smell of
moulding roses, because she had been so involved with
the dance and had forgotten not to breathe. For a long
time she had been in the habit of stopping to smell the
bouquets in the lounge. They seemed to be rotated week-
ly, sometimes more often. And more than once she had
wondered where they came from, who the anonymous
philanthropist might be since there were never any florist
cards attached to the flowers. She had speculated and
wondered until the day Tessie Bishop had caught her
sniffing and told her, "They come from funeral
parlours. Kind of nice of them to think of us," she said

"in time of sorrow and all." Most of the ladies really liked the bouquets. Arla heard them comment on the variety of colour of the blossoms from time to time in conversation before prayers. But she had hated the flowers ever since the day she talked to Tessie. Had always remembered not to breathe.

But there was magic in this dance. She couldn't deny it, in spite of the flowers and the forgetting not to breathe. She and Mrs. Dawson wheeling carefully and secretly around the chairs of the lodge lounge.

What delighted Arla most was the strength of the rhythm. Although the old woman had assumed the physical position of the female partner, there was no doubt in Arla's mind that she led, a definite sweep two-three, sweep two-three, turn two-three, step two-three. She never missed a beat. At the end of the dance, she chuckled, satisfied, then lifted the hem of her long black skirt in a mute and niggardly curtsey.

"Thank you, chicken," she said. "It's not everyone lives to be a hundred you know." She laughed again. "Good enough reason for dancin', I figure — not that I ever needed much of a reason. You look like you was brought up proper. You're a dancer, ain't ya?" Arla smiled. "Not many of the young folk know the old steps, you know." She lifted her skirt again and looked at her feet, thoughtfully, puzzled. Then she looked up at Arla quickly, "You polka?" she asked.

Arla laughed. "Yes," she said, "I polka."

Arla thought later that what Mrs. Dawson had said was so — not everyone did live to be a hundred. No one knew better than Arla that hardly anyone did.

With the others Arla had learned to accept, with in-difference almost, that incidents such as Mrs. Dawson's fall were like the top of a toboggan run for these old women. Once the toboggan slipped off the top, there was nowhere to go but down and swiftly. She had learned to hang on, brace herself, and wait. With Mrs. Dawson it was different.

Preparing the medications for breakfast, she began to doubt the report in the communications book. The night nurse, Mrs. Tittler, was herself older than many of the ladies in the lodge. She was absent-minded and tended to exaggerate. Mrs. Tittler, in fact, lost her upper plate more often on the night shift than any of the ladies ever did. Some mornings, Arla would find the teeth beside the sink faucets in the bathroom; sometimes they would be lodged between the cushions of a sofa in the lounge and one of the ladies would sit on them at prayer meeting and hold them up for identification and they belonged to no one present; so they were Mrs. Tittler's, again.

By the time she placed the last pills in the last small white cardboard cup on the medication tray, she had convinced herself that there was nothing seriously wrong with Mrs. Dawson. She decided to look in on the old woman before delivering the medications to the breakfast tables.

Mrs. Dawson was still in bed. An omen. Arla had never in all the time she had worked at the lodge found Mrs. Dawson in bed. She was always dressed and had her bed made by the time Arla arrived for the morning shift. She sat primly in an old armchair she had brought in from the farm at Cochrane. Sometimes she was crocheting. Sometimes she read the Bible. Her white hair was combed neatly back and pinned in a compact bun at the back of her head. Wire-frame spectacles perched at the end of her nose. She looked as if she had been up for hours.

Arla stood at the door, remembering, trying to fit her thoughts to what she actually saw. She surveyed the room, the rows upon rows of Christmas cards hung on strings against the far wall, the bureau with its wooden box of combs and hairpins, the chair by the window, and finally, the bed. Yes, Mrs. Dawsonn was still in bed. Her eyes were closed.

At first Arla thought she might already be dead, that the wait might be spared, but when she approached, the head on the pillow stirred and began to mutter, incoherently at first.

"Isabel," it said, "is that you dear? Is that you?"

"No," Arla replied quietly, "this is Arla, Mrs. Dawson, the day nurse. How are you?"

"I'm not too well dear, not well at all. Draw the drapes will you, Izzy? The sun's too blessed bright this morning. Why don't it ever get up at a decent hour?"

"Yes," said Arla, "I'll do that right now," though she knew there was no sun. Darkness stood like a sentinel in the long windowpane. Arla reached for the tassel and drew the blind.

She went back to the bed and switched on the bedside lamp. In the thin light she saw the ravages of the night just passed. Mrs. Dawson's face was at any time small but it looked minute this morning, separate from her body and almost from her head. She must have fallen forward and knocked her head. Her left eye was swollen, circled blue and black and yellow. Parts of her face were bandaged with thick white adhesive, sticky with blood on the edges, fresh blood. Arla winced.

How could anyone, even stupid inept Mrs. Tittler, put adhesive on this skin, this parchment? How would they ever get it off, even with alcohol? Yet Arla knew it had to come off — the wounds beneath were bleeding and a proper dressing had to be applied. Mrs. Tittler hadn't even used gauze, Arla noticed, let alone Telfa. She had stuck the adhesive directly to the cuts. Arla took a deep breath. She would see to this job later, after breakfast.

As she was closing the door, she noticed the blood on the pillowcase, dry and dark red near Mrs. Dawson's nose. She saw where the dry red trickle had left off from the old woman's cheek and dropped onto the linen. The linen would have to be changed too, she thought.

Well, that part was in fact true. The old woman had fallen. She had a nosebleed. She was muttering incoherently. But Arla resolved that she wouldn't let her die. Properly cared for, Arla reasoned, Mrs. Dawson would get better. She'd be sitting up in her old armchair, telling Arla stories again, stories full of secrets, clues to her longevity, her innocent happiness, the source of her calm and optimism and self-reliance. And if Arla had anything to say about it, she'd be dancing the day of her birth.

Arla never thought of Mrs. Dawson as she did the other lodge ladies. When she got her ring, all of the other ladies had said she was too young, she was just a girl, she was throwing her life away. Did she want to be tied down so early in life? Did she know what she was letting herself in for? No, they shook their heads ruefully; just an ignorant girl, how could she? "You'll see," they had said. "You'll find out that life's no bed of roses."

Mrs. Dawson had taken her hand and stroked the People's Credit ring as if through her fingertips she could feel the dazzle of light in the small stone and more important, as if she knew of the light which danced inside Arla. It was as if she knew that this stone was only a dull imitation of Arla's hope.

She had said she was happy for Arla, had stood back and really looked at her as if she were important, as if her plans were part of the fabric of the whole world and were therefore significant. And best of all, she had regarded Arla thoughtfully and said, "Yes, I had a companion once. We were together for forty years, and they were good years, good years."

Companion. That was the word Arla lifted out and turned over and over in her mind, studying it from every angle, like the ring. That was a good word. Sane and gentle and reassuring. She found herself taking the word out whenever she started to worry about David and their future together. Companion. It was all a matter of perspective, she thought. Some comfort there.

Just before Christmas Mrs. Dawson had crocheted a doily for Arla and folded it up inside a Christmas card on which she had written, "For your future, dear. Thank you to a good helper for all her kindness." Arla took it home to Saskatchewan at Christmas to show her folks. "A ninety-nine year-old woman made this, Mom," she said. "She'll be a hundred next month. Never say die, eh, Dad?" But what she really hoped was that they would read the card where it said, "Thank you to a good helper —," that they would know she was of some use to someone, had done something honourable with herself.

But they hadn't been impressed, not half as impressed as they were with the size of the diamond. She had watched her father finger the doily. Fingers had become

very important to her lately, especially David's. She
wished she was with him right now, wished it were summer, just she and David in the sun on the balcony of
her apartment, his rough fingers on her thigh. But she
wasn't. She was at Pine Mountain. Still she noticed
fingers and hands, even here. She remembered Mrs.
Dawson's fingers now hidden beneath the covers. The
old woman wore a thick gold band on the third finger
of her left hand. Arla had noticed it one day while watching her crochet.

At home, Arla had watched her father pass the doily
to her mother, who held it up to the light, examining the
web of crocheted yarn. ''It's a variation of the
'Snowflake,' '' she said. ''I got the same pattern. God,
I hope I can still function like that when I get to be her
age.'' Well, at least she had been properly impressed
with Mrs. Dawson's handiwork, thought Arla, but her
main interest was still the diamond.

''Biggest chunk of ice I ever saw,'' her mother had
said. ''You're a lucky little lady. Looks like you're gonna
be pretty well fixed.'' Remembering, Arla was filled with
doubt and apprehension, looked down at the stone,
turned it around once with the fingers of her right hand.
She didn't want to be ''fixed,'' well or any other way.

Before breakfast, Arla rushed from one room to
another, pinning a bun here, tying a shoelace there, pulling dark brown stockings up over hairless white, stick-
like legs. She coaxed and urged and even sometimes
teased the other ladies while she was working with them.
She was unusually thankful for the tedious routine, the
labyrinthine ins and outs of the lodge bedrooms and bath-
rooms and closets. At least she didn't have to think about
Mrs. Dawson. She could believe that everything was the

same as it had been hundreds of other mornings.

But when all the ladies were at breakfast and Mrs. Langland had been fed on the porch, Arla went straight to Mrs. Dawson, not dutifully but compulsively, and was shocked to find her exactly as she had left her. Again she saw the blood oozing out from underneath the adhesive tape and she reprimanded herself. She should have changed the dressing right away — she was sure she shouldn't have left it till now. And with the same certainty she began to understand that the old woman would definitely die, regardless of what she did.

She went to the medication cupboard in the kitchen and took out the things she would need — alcohol, sterile swabs, Telfa pads, tweezers, salve, Merthiolate. She arranged the supplies on a metal tray.

When she got back to the room she set the tray on the bedside table, pulled the arm chair over to the bed and reached to pull the blind tassel at the window. The blind rolled up rapidly, disappearing with a flap flap into wherever it is blinds go, into nowhere, it had always seemed to Arla, like time, like life.

The sunrise had begun and the pale window eye changed rapidly to a sparkle frosted paradise. The sun rose quickly through a thin layer of cloud, and with it rose Arla's anger. She began to remove the adhesive tape from the worst wound on the old woman's forehead. Just as she expected, the tissue paper skin came away with the tape. The old woman, barely conscious now, didn't move, but moaned throughout the whole grisly procedure. The cuts weren't deep but the removal of the skin made them look like moist red maps laced over pus-yellow flesh.

Arla clenched her teeth, nailed her mouth shut. She

thought about Mrs. Tittler, the stupid old fool. She cursed her, vowed she would report the matter, knowing all the while how useless that would be, what economic and sentimental defenses would be brought forth on behalf of the night nurse.

It wouldn't have been so bad if Mrs. Tittler's incompetence had been the only thing bothering her, feeding her anger. Arla couldn't help remembering her own mistakes. Everyone made them, regardless how hard a person tried not to. But why Mrs. Dawson, she kept thinking. Why not one of the cankerous old wretches in the lodge, one of the ones who made her life miserable, daily, reliably. It wasn't fair — anyone could tell that, especially this high-flown God, supposing there was one. She never said this, of course. She knew Mrs. Dawson was a believer.

The worst of it was she found herself furious with Mrs. Dawson, who lay motionless, though in pain. She wouldn't fight. Now she was giving up, after all those years, all those hard times she had come through and told stories about. Arla couldn't understand her own gullibility. She had believed in the old woman, put her faith in her. And what was she now but a quitter, nothing but a traitor.

Then she felt ashamed of herself. It wasn't Mrs. Dawson's fault she was dying. It wasn't even Mrs. Tittler's fault really, she knew that. For some inexplicable reason, she was sure it was, at least partly, her own fault. She should have been able to do something, get somebody else to do something. There should have been a way. That was what she was hired for, wasn't it. Maybe she wasn't very good at this job. Maybe if she had spoken up earlier about Mrs. Tittler's incompetence, none of this would have happened. But even while she thought of all these things, she knew that none of them gave her any answers.

Mrs. Dawson's nose had begun to bleed again and Arla brought her a cold cloth and placed it on her forehead before leaving. A nosebleed, she thought, a simple nosebleed. Could there be a more ridiculous way to die.

But her anger subsided a little as she walked through the corridor and into the lodge office to pick up the morning newspapers from the secretary's desk. Miss Piedmont wasn't in yet and everything still looked orderly in the office. Reassurance and a sense of continuation lay in the neat piles of paper in the "In" box on the desk.

On her way back to the dietary kitchen, Arla stopped to tell the matrons she wouldn't be coming to prayers. Mrs. Dawson was worse. The nosebleed had begun again.

"That's fine," said Matron Benstone, "thank you for letting us know. We called Dr. Jeremy and he said he'd drop by this afternoon. He advised us to notify her family in Cochrane."

"This afternoon!" Arla protested. "This afternoon could be too late."

"Well, he said he probably couldn't do much for her. After all, Arla, she's almost a hundred years old. We all have to go, Arla. Our time here is limited. The Lord will be waiting for Mrs. Dawson."

Arla turned and left. "That's the limit," she muttered to herself in the hallway. "That has to be the limit. All that malarky about the so-called Lord when really they don't give a damn, when it comes right down to it." Not if you really looked at the place, she thought. It reminded her of a holding pen.

She stopped to pick up fresh linen from the hall closet, then went to Mrs. Dawson's room. Nearing the bed, she reached out and touched the old woman's arm. "I'd like to change your bed, Mrs. Dawson," she said, "and make you a bit more comfortable."

But when the old lady tried to raise her head to answer, a river of bright red blood ran down her face and over her mouth. It divided into separate streams that ran down and around her chin. Arla grabbed a towel from the rung on the bedside table, placed it carefully under the old woman's nose and eased her back onto the pillow which by now was multi-coloured with white and orange and bright red and older, darker red.

Even so, the change of linen would have to wait. "You lie back now," Arla said. "We'll beat this nosebleed, Mrs. Dawson. You'll see. We'll have you back on your feet in no time. In lots of time for your party."

"No Izzy," Mrs. Dawson whispered. "There's goin' to be no partying around here till we're finished with chores. Now you run and tell Ray to get that water up to the house before I lose all my patience." her voice disappeared into a funnel of silence.

"Listen, just listen to me," Arla pleaded, "you're going to be all right. You got lots of life in you yet. We'll get you better." And then she blurted, "Where's all that fight, all that 'pioneer spirit' you told me about?"

By now Arla was stooped over the bed, her hands softly cupping the old woman's face, looking hard at the eyes, desperately trying to reach into that space which housed the fight, the will the old woman had brought over from the old country and had worked for years like a plough horse in order to get through all she had.

The woman's eyes glittered like blue ice in sun. "I

don't need it no more, don't want it no more. Can't you see, Izzy,'' she stammered, ''I'm going back — I'm ready — for the arms —''

Arms of the Lord. Absurd, thought Arla. She dropped the old woman's head quickly, as if it were a hot coal. She raised herself, drew back from the bed and in quiet horror regarded the head, moaning, whining for release from itself. She couldn't believe her ears, her eyes, and worse, the unavoidable truth. The old woman wanted to die — desired death like a lover, like a friend. Like Arla desired David.

In any case, she had things to do. She would at least change the incontinent pads on the old woman, the draw sheet on the bed. She could smell the urine as she unrolled the bedclothes, discovered the woman was wet but that was all. An easy change. She tucked the draw sheet under the soiled one, rolling the soiled one toward the body. Then she expertly shifted the body toward her, reached under it, grabbed both sheets, tugged the wet one out, threw it back onto the chair, and drew the clean sheet to the other side of the bed.

As she tucked the clean draw sheet tightly under the mattress, she found herself singing, then realized she was singing what the others were singing down the hall at the prayer meeting. ''Rock of ages, cleft for me, Let me hide myself in Thee; Let the water and the blood —'' She stopped abruptly and rolled the bedclothes up and over the old woman's withered frame, now curled into the foetal position. Again only the head was showing above the blankets. Arla had to leave. A person had to go to the bathroom regardless of what was going on, she reasoned.

On her way back she passed the lounge where the other

ladies had been gathered for their prayer meeting. She
looked in through the doorway. The room was empty
now but a curious, chill feeling came over her. For only
a moment she thought she saw Mrs. Dawson dancing
with someone. Later, she tried to tell David about it, tried
to remember the face of Mrs. Dawson's partner and
couldn't. She knew she was foolish to worry about it.
It was obviously a figment of her imagination. But at
the time, she had seen his features very clearly, as clearly
as Mrs. Dawson's.

And she remembered that the old woman had been
gay and smiling. And the melody of the song kept running through her head, and the words — as if she were
actually hearing them, ''I was waltzing with my darling
to the Tennessee waltz, when an old friend I happened
to see; I introduced him to my loved one, and while they
were dancing, my friend stole my sweetheart from me.
I remember the —''

At first Arla wouldn't go back to the old woman's
room. She was under a lot of pressure. That's all
it was, she reasoned with herself. Your mind played funny tricks on you when you were upset. She was upset
— that's all it was.

She felt sad, suddenly very sad and heavy, as if she
were carrying something large and solid, needed to walk
slowly, to be steady. She hesitated for a minute in front
of the door, then forced herself to open it.

The old woman lay still in the bed. Arla lowered herself
into the old farm chair and began to wait. Finally she
looked at her watch and decided she'd better bath Mrs.
Torpor. Mrs. Torpor always took a long time to bath.
She was severely crippled with arthritis and Arla had
to use the hoyer.

But when she stood to leave, she was startled by a violent movement in the bed. The old woman sat incredibly upright, calling ''Lord, Lord, Lord, take me —'' and Arla responded by lurching toward the bed and grabbing hold of the body and holding onto it tightly as though it would have climbed out and run down the hall had she let go. She rocked it and rocked it and rocked it. Humming and rocking, humming and rocking. And at some point — for it seemed to her afterward to have been a specific, clearly defined point in time — Arla felt as if she and the old woman had changed partners. But Arla couldn't let her go right away. By the time her arms relaxed and she lowered the body to the linen, her face was clammy and wet and the remnant flesh on the bed had begun to stiffen, to grow cold. She reached down and closed the eyelids with the tips of her fingers.

She looked up, focused her eyes on the rows and rows of Christmas cards on strings against the far wall. It would be a big funeral but she had already decided she wouldn't go.

The collar and one sleeve of her uniform were stained with blood. She'd have to change it before she went to the other ladies, would have to borrow a uniform from one of the matrons. How could she have known about today, any more than all the others. Slowly, as if through water, she reached for the tassel on the blind and drew it down over the window, still live with sparkle frost.

She pulled the top sheet up and over the head of the body which now appeared completely peaceful, though uninhabited. She closed the door quietly when she left the room and without looking back, she went to tell the matron that it was over, that Mrs. Dawson had died.

''I quit,'' she said, quite without warning to herself.

"I beg your pardon," said Matron Oliver, who was sitting behind the office desk beside Miss Piedmont. They were going over figures which Arla could see only upside-down in the ledger.

"I said I'm giving my notice," Arla said calmly.

"Listen dear, I'll take care of arrangements for Mrs. Dawson." The matron was moving toward Arla, reaching out to put her arms around her, but Arla backed away.

"It doesn't matter," she said, "I'll do it." In a way she was sorry she had said it, remembered the other lodgers who had died while she was on duty, remembered every one gone since she had come to work at Pine Mountain. Remembered her fingers on their eyes, bathing their bodies, stuffing their dark mouths and anuses full of cotton. "I'm quitting anyway," she said.

"But what will you do?" asked the matron, gentle now.

"I don't know," said Arla, "but I'll find something."

For one thing, she thought as she turned to leave the office, she could move in with David until she found another job. They were together all the time anyway and he had been asking her to move in for months. The fact was she wanted to live with him, and right now she couldn't think of a single reason why not. Needing someone didn't make you weak. It made you human. But walking down the long hallway toward Mrs. Dawson's room, she began to finger the diamond ring on her right hand. She rotated it a couple of times, then slipped it off and shoved it into her uniform pocket. She didn't give a damn about it. She might as well face the fact that she didn't give a damn about the ring. As far as she was concerned they should take it back to People's and get their money back. Maybe buy a decent bed. David only had a roll-a-way. She would talk to him about it tonight.

At the end of the shift she put on her coat. She took off her duty shoes, left them in a corner of the closet, and put on her boots. When the afternoon nurse came to relieve her, she left by the sun porch door, walked out into the snow which was still falling in large white lazy flakes, still clinging to the cloth of her coat.

On the street she found herself singing the Tennessee Waltz, almost out loud. She looked over her shoulder, furtively, not so much because she felt foolish and was afraid someone had heard her singing, but because she felt she was not alone, because she felt the presence of someone or something walking with her.

Carol Shields

VARIOUS MIRACLES: A ROUNDUP

Several of the miracles that occured in the year 1983 have gone unrecorded.

Example: On the morning of January 3, seven women stood in line at a lingerie sale in Palo Alto, California, and by chance each of these women bore the Christian name Emily.

Example: On February 16th four strangers (three men, one woman) sat quietly reading on the back seat of the number 10 bus in Cincinnati, Ohio; each of them was reading a paperback copy of SMILEY'S PEOPLE and each happened to be on page 279.

On March 30th a lathe operator in a Moroccan mountain village dreamt that a lemon fell from a tree into his open mouth, causing him to choke and die. He opened his eyes, overjoyed at being still alive, and embraced his wife who was snoring steadily by his side. She scarcely stirred, being reluctant to let go of the dream she was dreaming, which was that a lemon tree had taken root in her stomach, sending its pliant new shoots upwards into her limbs. Leaves, blossoms, and finally fruit fluttered in her every vein until she began to tremble in her sleep with happiness and intoxication. Her husband got up quietly and lit an oil lamp so that he could watch her face. It seemed to him he had never really looked at her before and he felt how utterly ignorant he was of the spring that nourished her life. Now she lay sleeping, dreaming, her face radiant. What he saw was a mask of happiness so intense it made him fear for his life.

On May 11th, in the city of Exeter in the south of England, five girls (aged 15 to 17) were running across a playing field at ten o'clock in the morning as part of their physical education program. They stopped short when they saw, lying on the broad gravel path, a dead parrot. He was grassy green in colour with a yellow nape and head, and was later identified by the girls' science mistress as *Amazona ochrocephala*. The police were notified of the find and later it was discovered that the parrot had escaped from the open window of a house owned by a Mr. and Mrs. Ramsay who claimed, while weeping openly, that they had owned the parrot (Miguel by name) for twenty-two years. The parrot, in fact, was twenty-five years old, one of a pair of birds sold in an open market in Marseilles in the spring of 1958. Miguel's twin brother was sold to an Italian soprano who kept it for ten years, then gave it to her niece Francesca, a violinist who played first with the Netherlands Chamber Orchestra and later with the Chicago Symphony. On May 11th Francesca was wakened in her River Forest home by the sound of her parrot (Pete, or sometimes Pietro) coughing. She gave him a dish of condensed milk instead of his usual whole oats-and-peanut mixture, and then she phoned to say she would not be able to attend rehearsal that day. The coughing grew worse. She looked up the name of a vet in the Yellow Pages and was about to dial when the parrot fell over, dead in his cage. A moment before Francesca had heard him open his beak and pronounce what she believed were the words, "*Ca ne fait rien.*"

On August 26th a man named Carl Hallsbury of Billings, Montana was wakened by a loud noise. "My God, we're being burgled," his wife Marjorie said. They listened, but when there were no further noises, they drifted back to sleep. In the morning they found that their favourite little watercolour — a pale rural scene depicting trees and a winding road and the usual arched bridge — had fallen off the livingroom wall. It appeared that it had bounced onto the cast iron radiator and then ricocheted to a safe place in the middle of the livingroom rug. When Carl investigated he found that the hook had worked loose in the wall. He patched the plaster methodically, allowed it to dry, and then installed a new hook. While he worked he remembered how the picture had come into his possession. He had come across it hanging in an emptied-out house in the French city of St. Brieuc where he and the others of his platoon had been quartered during the last months of the war. The picture appealed to him, its simple lines and the pale tentativeness of the colours. In particular the stone bridge caught his attention since he had been trained as a civil engineer (Purdue, 1939). When orders came to vacate the house late in 1944, he popped the little watercolour into his knapsack; it was a snug fit, and the snugness seemed to condone his theft. He was not a natural thief but already he knew that life was mainly a matter of improvisation. Other returning soldiers brought home German helmets, strings of cartridge shells and flags of various sorts, but the little painting was Carl's only souvenir. And his wife Marjorie is the only one in the world who knows it to be stolen goods; she and Carl belong to a generation that believed there should be no secrets between married couples. Both of them, Marjorie as much as Carl, have a deep sentimental attachment to the picture, though they no longer believe it to be the work of a skilled artist.

It was, in fact, painted by a twelve-year-old boy named Pierre Renaud who until 1943 had lived in the St. Brieuc house. It was said that as a child he had a gift for painting and drawing; in fact, he had a gift merely for imitation. His little painting of the bridge was copied from a postcard his father sent him from Burgundy where he had gone to conduct some business. Pierre had been puzzled and ecstatic at receiving a card from his parent, who was a cold, resolute man with little time for his son. The recopying of the postcard in watercolours — later Pierre saw all this clearly — was an act of pathetic homage, almost a way of petitioning his father's love.

He grew up to become not an artist but a partner in the family leather goods business. In the late summer he likes to go south in pursuit of sunshine and good wine, and one evening, the 26th of August it was, he and Jean-Louis, his companion of many years, found themselves on a small stone bridge not far from Tournus. "This is it," he announced excitedly, spreading his arms like a boy, and not feeling at all sure what he meant when he said the words, "This is it." Jean-Louis gave him a fond smile; everyone knew Pierre had a large capacity for nostalgia. "But I though you said you'd never been here before," he said. "That's true," Pierre said, "you are right. But I feel, *here*" — he pointed to his heart — "that I've stood here before." Jean-Louis teased him by saying, "Perhaps it was in another life." Pierre shook his head, "No, no, no," and then, "well, perhaps." After that the two of them stood on the bridge for some minutes regarding the water and thinking their separate thoughts.

On October 31st Camilla LaPorta, a Cuban-born writer, now a Canadian citizen, was taking the manuscript of her new novel to her Toronto publisher on Front Street. She was nervous; the publisher had been critical of her first draft, telling her it relied too heavily on the artifice of coincidence. Camilla had spent many months on revision, plucking apart the faulty tissue that joined one episode to another, and then, delicately, with the pains of a neurosurgeon, making new connections. The novel now rested on its own complex micro-circuitry. Wherever fate, chance or happenstance had ruled, there was now logic, causality and science.

As she stood waiting for her bus on the corner of College and Spadina that fall day, a gust of wind tore the manuscript from her hands. In seconds the yellow typed sheets were tossed into a whirling dance across the busy intersection. Traffic became confused. A bus skittered on an angle. Passersby were surprisingly helpful, stopping and chasing the blowing papers. Several sheets were picked up from the gutter where they lay on a heap of soaked yellow leaves. One sheet was found plastered against the windshield of a parked Pontiac half a block away; another adhered to the top of a lamppost; another was run over by a taxi and bore the black herringbone of tire prints. From all directions, ducking the wind, people came running up to Camilla and bringing her the scattered pages. "Oh this is crazy, this is crazy," she cried into the screaming wind.

When she got to the publisher's office he took one look at her manuscript and said, "Good God Almighty, don't tell me, Camilla, that you of all people have become a post-modernist and no longer believe in the logic of page numbers."

Camilla explained about the blast of wind, and then the two of them began to put the pages in their proper order. Astonishingly, only one page was missing, but it was a page which Camilla insisted was pivotal, a keystone page, the page that explained everything else. She would have to try to reconstruct it as best she could. "Hmmmm," the publisher said — this was late in the afternoon of the same day and they sat in the office sipping tea — "I truly believe, Camilla, that your novel stands up without the missing page. Sometimes, you know, it's better not to explain everything. Sometimes it's better to let things be strange and to represent nothing but themselves."

The missing page — it happened to be page 46 — had blown around the corner of College Street into the open doorway of a fresh fruit and vegetable shop where a young woman in a red coat was buying a kilo of zucchini. It happend that she was very beautiful, though not in a conventional way. She was also talented, an actress, who for some months had been out of work. To give herself courage and to cheer herself up she had decided to make a batch of zucchini-oatmeal muffins, and she was just counting out the change on the counter when the sheet of yellow paper blew through the doorway and landed at her feet.

She was the kind of young woman who loves to read; she reads everything, South American novels, Russian folktales, Persian poetry, the advertisements on the subway, the personal column in the *Globe and Mail,* even the Instructions and Precautions on public fire extinguishers. Print is her way of entering and escaping the world. It was only natural for her to bend over and pick up the yellow sheet and begin to read.

She read: *A woman in a red coat is standing in a grocery store buying a kilo of zucchini. She is beautiful, though not in a conventional way, and it happens that she is an actress who —*

Diane Schoemperlen

LIFE SENTENCES

They've known each other, this woman, this man,
ever since they were kids, healthy, wealthy and (   ).
For all their young lives, they lived in identical ranch-
style homes side by side on West (   ) Avenue. Both
their fathers were important energetic men in the (   )
Company downtown and their mothers were (   )
housewives, lazy and slim.

They were both only children, growing up smoothly
with a strong sense of their own (   ) power.
Everywhere they looked, there was money, or signs of
it. Money was not something they ever had to (   )
about. They lived comfortable lucky lives, exclusive,
(   ) lives. They knew nothing of pain or suffering,
danger of (   ). Such things did not seem (   ) or
possible.

As adults, they share (   ) memories of lavish turkey dinners, shiny bicycles, picnics at the cottage on Lake (   ), and washing the Cadillacs with their dads on Saturday afternoon in the sunshine. Their moms are sitting in one kitchen or the other, slopping up brandy until they come outside, angry and squinting and (   ), refusing to cook. These kids don't care, they don't know any (   ).

They were innocent together, this girl, this boy. They have no sense now of having met; they might as well have been (   ), that's how close they were.

One day in high school the young woman looked (   ) at the young man and saw that he was remarkable. She knew then that she wanted to spend the rest of her (   ) with him and only him. There was no reason to think that she wouldn't. She'd always got what she (   ) before.

They did everything together in those halcyon days and their parents thought they were (   ) and cute. They went to movies, dances and football parties, holding (   ), smiling and kissing in corners. They made (   ) love in the back seat of the car the young man's parents bought him for his (   ) birthday. The young woman loved it when he put his (   ) in her (   ). She was filling up her hope chest with crystal, fine linen and (   ). She just naturally assumed that the young man (   ) her as much as she (   ) him. He certainly (   ) as if he did.

Of course their parents all approved. Their fathers were talking about retiring early and buying a condo in (   ), which was all the rage at the time. Their mothers were still drunk half the time and now these two kids understood that such behaviour was (   ) and likely to drive them to the same psychiatrist in later years.

After high school, the young man smashed up his car and walked away without a (   ) to some fancy college in (   ). The young woman stayed behind and sold novels in a bookstore while she (   ) for him to come home. Her rich parents said this lousy job was (   ) for her.

They wrote letters back and forth, this young woman, this young man, long letters, (   ) letters, unsatisfying letters. It was only after the young man came home for Christmas the second year with a (   ) gypsy girl that the young woman realized he might not (   ) her after all. Some men, when you (   ) them, you just know that somehow, slowly, they're going to defeat you. She was (   ), but he wasn't paying attention anymore. So she pretended to be (   ) and succeeded. He was (   ) fooled.

The man and the gypsy were married the next summer in his parents' backyard. The woman was invited of course and had to go just to show him she wasn't (   ).

But the young woman still (   ) the young man. She got fat, fat, fatter, sad, sad, sadder, and her broken heart was driving her (   ). So her worried parents sent her away to Europe for a little (   ). She came home much thinner and much (   ). She hated the young man now, which was much easier than (   ) him.

In a few years, the young woman, who was no longer feeling young, married a doctor who (   ) her desperately and bought her a mansion filled with wonderful things right on (   ) Street, the best part of town. Her parents didn't really like this doctor but they figured he was better than (   ). So did the woman. She didn't really (   ) this doctor but figured she'd learn to in time. The young man was (   ) and didn't make it to the wedding. He sent along a Cuisinart instead. The young woman's parents thought that was the end of that. Not likely, not by a (   ) shot.

Shortly afterwards, the young man's father (   ) himself tragically in the head, his mother promptly (   ) herself to death, and the young man inherited everything, through no (   ) of his own. He had so much money then, he would never have to work again. It was all very (   ).

As it turned out, the mansion he bought for his gypsy wife happened to be on the same street as the mansion of the woman and her doctor husband. He said it was an accident, purely (   ). By now he had a set of gypsy twins and another (   ) on the way. He was always buying new Cadillacs and smashing them up, a ridiculous habit that nobody (   ) seriously. He was just like a cat with (   ) lives, extended lives, flaunting them. The woman had become a writer of (   ) poetry and no longer found it necessary to (   ) the man. She was writing about other things now anyway. Absence makes the (   ) grow (   ). They were both getting older and (   ), in spite of themselves.

So they decided to become friends again, (   ) at first and then (   ). Pretty soon, it was as though they'd never been (   ).

The man teaches the doctor how to (   ) and, in return, the doctor teaches the man how to (   ). They have many things in (   ), the two men discover. They love the same restaurant, the same sports, the same (   ). After a while, they even begin to (   ) alike.

Sometimes the woman babysits the gypsy twins and

the new baby, who is a (   ). She has never liked kids but it seems the (   ) she can do for that (   ) woman. She and the gypsy go shopping together, drink (   ), laugh about (   ) and talk about (   ). Everyone thinks the two women are (   ) friends and in a way they are, too.

The woman and the man are glad to be (   ) again after all that's happened. They tell each other (   ) and they kiss in corners on New Year's Eve. Once or twice the doctor accuses the woman of having an (   ) with the man but of course that isn't strictly true. Still though, he says she just wants to have her (   ) and eat it too.

One day at lunch the man confessed to the woman that his marriage was (   ). The woman was hardly surprised — indeed, this seemed in retrospect to be exactly what she'd (   ) all along. The gypsy said the man was a (   ). The man said the gypsy was a (   ). They would never be (   ) again so there was no use trying. It was nobody's fault.

Not long afterwards, the doctor announced he was in (   ) with the gypsy. Everybody was surprised but there was (   ) to be done about it now. The doctor said the woman had never really (   ) him. The woman said that was true, (   ) but true. There was no one to blame. They were all very civilized people, unlucky maybe, but (   ).

After the divorces, which were unfriendly but (   ), the man and the woman stuck together. It was the (   ) thing to do. They (   ) each other.

The woman soon sold her mansion and moved all her furniture down the street. The gypsy's furniture was (   ) anyway, so they sold it. The woman wanted to burn it but the man said she was being (   ).

By this time, the woman's parents had moved down south to the dream condo in (   ) and she was glad she no longer had to face them. Her psychiatrist had helped her understand that she would never be able to (   ) them, no matter what she did. It was the curse of only children that their parents were never (   ), never satisfied.

This same psychiatrist had also helped the man realize he would never be happy either and his trouble with those Cadillacs was a (   ) wish. They were working on their problems (   ), this woman, this man, and it was no wonder they had so many, considering the way their (   ) mothers had (   ) them.

The man and the woman had all the same friends as before and nobody seemed to (   ) that the doctor and the gypsy had disappeared. It was as though those other two had never been much (   ) anyway. There was no need to get married now: once bitten, twice (   ). Besides, they were too old to have (   ) now anyway — it was too late for some things, lots of things, (   ) things.

Their lives, twin lives, discoloured, go on and on and always (   ). They still like to (   ) and (   ) and (   ). They still love the same(   ), the same (   ), and the same (   ). The man is still buying Cadillacs, and the woman is still writing poetry. She knows that they're supposed to be (   ) at last. What more could they (   ) for? But her poems are all about (   ) and the man just wrecked another one.

Today the man is out in the driveway washing the Cadillac. The woman is thinking that if she has to watch him do this one more time she will (   ), just (   ). She's in the kitchen drinking (   ) and getting meaner and (   ) by the minute. She knows this drinking is a (   ) habit. She knows she's just like her (   ). How depressing, how (   ), how true.

It seems that there are only two more things she can do in her life: stay with this man till (   ) freezes over or (   ) him. He'd be better off (   ) anyway.

Either way, she knows she will never be free of him. This man does not (   ) her, she knows that now, she's sure he never did, she's sure he never will. He knows her too well, all too (   ). Familiarity breeds (   ). She keeps wishing he'd drive the new Cadillac over a cliff and be (   ) with it. She can just see the flames, she can just hear the (   ), she can almost taste the gallons of (   ). The one thing she has never been in her life is alone.

She goes through all the ways she could do it, one by one. The possibilities are (   ). She thinks that (   ) would be best — bloodless, tidy and (   ). No one will ever know. She's sure she'll get away with it — she'd lead a charmed life. No one will even (   ) her. She is above suspicion, though not above (   ).

The clouds are (   ), the ill wind is (   ), it looks like it's going to (   ).

Life, it seems from this vantage point, tends, intends, to go on for a very long time. There is no one to blame, no one to thank, no one but (   ).

Eunice Scarfe

IN THE CLEARING

And there is Emma on the path, pushing the pram, back and forth across the overgrown middle of the clearing, Emma pushing six bald heads, all open-mouthed, waiting to be fed. Emma feeds them song instead, little morsels of lyrics sung with impeccable inflection and quite unnecessary melodic excess. The children's mouths remain open. They want food. Six tiny siblings sitting in the elevated sling of a very proper pram. Between the edge of the damp woods and the brink of the steep hill, Emma is pushing the pram, casting a short shadow in the sunlight, moving back and forth. Would Emma prefer to push this pram around the soothing circumference of a dark and peaceful pond? She will never say. She sticks to this path, to the straightness of this path, pushing back and forth. How else could she be seen? If she were to walk in the woods, between the trees, or over there along the cliff, she might be altogether out of sight. No, Emma prefers the path. She loves a parade. There are no benches here and Emma would not use one even if there were. She would not wish to appear weary or in any way worn out by her baby-breeding activities. In her white skirt she continues to walk and to smile beneath her thickly wrapped crown of braided brown hair. The babies' mouths remain open. They want food. Emma, can't you hear them? They want food. Emma gives them song instead.

Jake is chopping wood. In the clearing, between the path and the cliff, he is chopping wood, bringing carefully planned strokes down upon the edge of the wood. The wood splits, cracks and falls along its appointed line. He stops between strokes to stretch and look around. He will see Emma and wave and she will stop and talk to him, all the while waiting for the others to arrive and to admire the expertise with which she pushes six bald babies in the haughty English pram. Jake's red and black wool shirt is torn over the sleeve, stained with oil, minus several buttons, and mended on the elbow with thick yellow thread. He wears it with pride. He is sure it is envied and understood by all who might see him in the clearing chopping wood so well. He stacks the wood carefully in a triangle of perfection, an evenly ascending line. No piece is any longer than the others. "My father," says Emma, stopping for a moment by his side, "cut his wood with a circular electric saw."

"My father," says Jake, "hired someone else to cut his wood."

"Oh," says Emma, moving off, "how very nice indeed."

Colin does not envy Jake his shirt. Colin is sitting under a tree with a bottle of Guinness in one hand and a bottle of Scotch in the other. He has forgotten which drink is chasing which. He sees Emma and wonders why she should be smiling, worse, singing. Such a full-bodied smile, such an able body, should be devoted to more energetic animal activity than pushing a finely sprung pram. He suspects she keeps herself with child in order to produce that fine full bosom. He remembers when she was a skinny stick of a girl, as flat-chested as he, and now the handle of the pram is hidden by her ballooning breasts. He would like to drink from them just once, a chaser to the Scotch which is quickly running out. He would kneel to reach those breasts of hers. If he stood, his thick black hair would scrape the branches of the Douglas fir.

Ah, Emma. Do you see Colin sitting under the tree? Are you going to wave to him? Are you going to stop and talk?

Along the path Amanda is walking out of the woods. Colin does not want to see Amanda. Amanda, like Emma, is good but Emma chooses goodness and Amanda cannot help herself. Amanda will say 'Hello.' She will not look at the bottles. She will not ask him why he drinks so early in the day, she will know. Has she brought some homemade cornbread in her hand? And is that coffee in the flask precariously perched in the pocket of the backpack where Jonathon sits with head thrown back watching silently the sky? Is she coming towards him? She is. She will not say much, she will listen, she will chuckle, not laugh, just a throaty rumble of contentment. Why should she subject him to the sounds of her contentment, Colin asks. Let him have the cornbread. Let him have the coffee. Let her go away. Right away.

Priscilla is picking pine cones. She has a step ladder
and a long tool with a handle to squeeze the cone should
one be unwilling to fall. She has brought three identical
baskets. She will put one hundred cones in each. Then
she will be finished. She will not stop for drinks of Scotch
or Guinness or even of milk until she is finished. There
is a job to be done here. There must be a plan. One hundred per basket gives her a chance to develop a trio of
a rhythm, a waltz of a routine. She will strip the south
side of the tree first, then the northeast and finally the
northwest. That should do the job. Priscilla is a little lady.
Her back is breaking and her eyes, lifted up to spot the
dark pine cones, are full of falling needles and bits of
dripping sap, but the job must be done and Priscilla is
the one to do it. Or is she?

Sharon comes striding out of the trees now, whistling,
swiftly manoeuvering her way between fallen logs and
clumps of overgrown grass. She wears Wellington boots,
a thickly-knit wool sweater, and baggy trousers rolled
up as far as her knees. She takes one look at Priscilla
and says, "Here, let me help you."

Sharon scales the tree, swiftly reaches the top, and
tosses a pine cone down to Priscilla before aiming one
each to Emma, Jake and Colin. Priscilla is hit squarely
between the eyes. Jake watches his land before slicing
it neatly in two with his axe. Emma tucks the pretty pine
cone in between her pretty babies' legs and Colin idly
watches the pine cone roll to a stop at his feet. Then
Sharon slowly descends, stripping every pine cone as she
comes. They fall in piles at Priscilla's tiny feet.

When Sharon swings herself down from the last branch
she faces a speechless Priscilla. Priscilla's routine has been

destroyed. Doesn't Sharon see that? No, Sharon does not. She laughs and does not go away. She stays right there and scoops those pine cones up with a shovel which she borrows from Jake. She piles then, dirt together with the cones, in the waiting empty baskets. Still Priscilla does not speak. "Where do you want these?" Sharon asks, lifting easily a basket to her shoulder. Still there is no answer. Sharon, shrugging, moves off and Priscilla, alone at last, begins again to count the cones.

Diana is pushing a pram as well. Her breasts are nowhere near the handle. They have returned to their original discreet and proportionate size. Her pram needs only one hand. In the other, she carries a boomerang. She tosses it in the direction of Jake, and the boomerang, whizzing skillfully through the trees, returns swiftly to Diana's outstretched and waiting hand. Only Colin sees her grin. He grins as well. Will she do it again? She will. She takes aim for Priscilla. Right over her head. If Priscilla had been standing, the boomerang would easily have decapitated her. Diana laughs again. Diana's daughter laughs as well and even claps her hands. Colin takes another swig of Scotch. He is enjoying this. Diana has a certain skill you might say, not quite that required for cricket or rugby, but impressive nevertheless. If the boomerang comes his way, he's going to interrupt the circle. He's going to catch her boomerang if it ever comes his way.

Pete has brought his little boy Joe and a fishing rod to keep them company. They head through the brush to the edge of the cliff. Two hundred feet of line will be necessary to fish from here. Two hundred feet of line is nothing. Joe watches patiently while Pete readies the line. Then both sit down, father and son together, backs

to the clearing, alone against the height of the limp blue
sky and do not turn around again.

Sharon ambles over. She will join Pete and Joe.

"Catch anything yet?"

"No, nothing yet."

"I'm not surprised."

"No, neither am I," answers Pete. "Care to have a
go?"

"Sure," says Sharon, taking the pole in her hand.

Now three sit with their backs to the clearing and their
eyes facing the empty sky.

Amanda has taken Jonathon from his backpack. Jake
puts away his axe and helps Jonathon make a train with
the even lengths of wood. Diana and her daughter join
them. They will make a city. Pine cones would be useful
but they will look for stones instead. They will use the
boomerang to mark the center of the city. Jonathon and
Diana's daughter work in silent concentration.

"Don't worry about the slivers," says Jake, "because
there aren't any. It's the way I chopped each piece."

"Slivers?" say the mothers simultaneously. "Why
would we be worried?"

From the woods at this moment comes a runner, his
emerald triple-ply polyester jersey suit stretched tightly
across his body, its smooth surface interrupted only by
tiny tubes which spray the salty sweat away from
him. His head is covered with a helmet in which an
ionizer is constantly at work. Emma sees him coming,
hesitates, and steps aside to let him pass. Priscilla, counting pine cones, looks up, loses track and must begin
again. Jake nods at Diana, who sends her boomerang
across the runner's path. It passes gracefully in front of
him and returns to Diana behind his back. Colin grins

again. Is this the messenger they have all been waiting for?

Just as the runner disappears from sight, Mary comes along wearing wide-bottomed jeans with even wider cuffs and hair cut in a severe circle around her round fat face. She looks puzzled.

"Why are you counting the pine cones?" she asks of Priscilla.

"Eighty-two, eight-three," continues Priscilla, looking up just once. Mary moves away.

"Can't you hear your babies crying?" Mary asks Emma as she meets her on the path. "Aren't you ever going to feed them anything?"

"Thank you for your suggestion," says Emma. "Perhaps I'll feed them now."

Emma props the babies up, three on a side. They face each other like two opposing teams. She leans forward over the pram. Six tits slip smoothly out of the soft whiteness of her wrap-around silk blouse. Six pairs of toothless gums suck noisily at once. Emma rests her chin on the canopy of the pram. "I haven't seen you down here before," she says to Mary.

"I haven't been here before," says Mary, "and I certainly haven't seen six at once before. I mean six on one. I mean are they all yours?" Mary can't take her eyes off Emma's multiple facilities.

"Yes, they're all mine," says Emma. "I'd never adopt someone else's child, would you?"

Mary leaves Emma and her busy noisy babies and walks towards the woodpile. "Why are you chopping wood?" Mary asks. Amanda and Diana look at Mary kindly. The children place sticks of wood up and over Mary's shoes in order to make a bridge. Jake begins to chop again.

"I don't understand," says Mary, "what everyone is doing here."

Mary approaches Sharon, Pete and Joe. "Can't you see there isn't any water? How do you expect to catch a fish?" Pete turns his head to look at her. Does not invite her to sit down. Certainly does not invite her to have a go. Joe snuggles closer to the safety of his daddy. Sharon speaks to Pete, "Should I hold it tightly do you think, or loosely in the arm, like this?"

"Like that," Pete says, "there you have it."

In the silence after Pete has finished speaking Mary moves away as quickly as she can.

Mary sees a man under the tree. He is lonely and unoccupied. She will sit with him. That would be a very nice thing to do. She walks towards him and catches a glint of glass. And then another and another. Bottles, bottles everywhere. She continues walking towards him until she sees his eyes are closed, his head thrown back. He is perhaps asleep. But is that a hand moving? Yes, it is his hand, moving back and forth, his hand fondly handling the firm white flesh of himself. Has he seen her? How can she get away? Should she turn, should she scream? Should she try and stop him? Mary turns and runs away.

Runs to the edge of the clearing where the clearing meets the cliff. Poised on the edge of the crumbling cliff she stands. Pine cones, carefully counted pine cones, pelt against her back and Mary, unbalanced, loses her footing and falls without a splash into the rocky river bed below. Brown cones bury her beneath their jagged sticky edges.

Silence in the clearing.

Emma's babies are asleep. Priscilla sits very still, beside her empty baskets, her face completely hidden by long blond hair. Colin walks alone into the woods. Amanda and Diana begin to build again the sliverless symmetry of Jake's pyramid of wood. And the children? The children chase each other calmly in the sun.

Up the hill, from the flat below the clearing, comes the runner now. He is moving in superb slow motion, his polyester costume shed in favour of crisp white cotton. His sweat is drying in the sun. The runner's head is high, his breathing easy, his eyes clear. His hair, dark and thick, moves easily around his head. Dressed all in white, the runner comes, an arrow moving along the straightness of the path.

The fishers on the cliff hear his footsteps. Emma's babies, sleeping, are pushed aside to let him pass. Priscilla lifts her head, untroubled by this interruption. The five squatting at the wood pile stand, one by one, to hear the runner speak.

The messenger, when he meets the middle of the clearing, stops and looks at each of those assembled here. The group is silent. ''Are you ready?'' the runner asks of them. And begins, in measured careful words, to speak so all can hear.

Caterina Edwards

QUIRKS AND QUARKS

"You have to tell me."

I lifted my head slowly as if I were being torn away from my notes against my will. "Tell you? What?"

"The truth . . ."

I begin the story at this point: James and I in my tiny, yellow-walled office, not because it was the beginning but because this banal scene is the first in the sequence of scenes that I have worried over in the intervening years, as I would worry over each significant step (the mathematical calculations, the equations and graphs) to an inconclusive, worse, a contradictory experiment, methodically reviewing, repeatedly searching for the error.

"I have to know," he said.

And I slowly rotated my chair, as if I were still

somewhere else, as if I hadn't been thinking all morning of him, of his dark eyes and his round little-boy head.

"You would know. She'd tell you. You'd be the one person who would know." He had pulled up the spare chair so he was close, his knees almost touched mine. "She has a lover, doesn't she? I figured it out. She's deceiving me." He was pulling out a pack of cigarettes, tearing the plastic, pulling at the top. All of his gestures were quick, impatient.

I passed him an ashtray, then let my hand fall casually on my notes. Probability waves, the mathematical catalogues of the tendency to happen. "I don't know why you men always have to be so melodramatic, paranoid. You should know Anne after all these years. She can't stand to feel caged. Try to stay rational. Besides, I thought you two didn't think in terms of deception." His habitual intense gaze did flicker but he didn't look away. "You keep saying you don't own each other. That your marriage is open. No repression. No compulsive monogamy." He was uncomfortable, shifting in his chair, preparing a defense. "No. I can't argue now. I have to finish my lecture: light, a wave or a particle." Anne, faithful or false. "Probability and *potentia*."

I had propelled my chair ever so slightly backwards, but he simply stretched out his legs further, again almost touching me.

"I'm not stupid. I know something's going on."

"But think how much easier it would make things for you. Ease your burden of guilt. That should make you question your interpretation of the data. 'The observed system cannot be observed until it interacts with the observing system.' How often have you repeated that to your students? How often have you complained to me that they willfully don't understand?''

His face lightened instantly. His old wry smile was back. ''Well, she can be so self-righteous.''

''Umm . . . look, we can have lunch in an hour. But right now I want to get back to the lecture. 'Potentia' — standing between the idea of an event and the actual event.''

'' 'Between possibility and reality'. That'll confuse their little minds.'' He was actually standing, butting his cigarette. ''I am so sick of all those blank little faces. I don't know how long I can stick at this job.''

''Well, it's an appropriate topic today, I think.''

I shouldn't have reminded him. His smile vanished. He dropped back into the chair. More, he grabbed my hand, forcing me to drop the pen I had just picked up. ''Please.''

I stared straight into his dark dark eyes. ''No, James, she doesn't have a lover. She doesn't.'' He let go.

''Thanks.'' He wanted to leave now. He was embarrassed.

''It's the last time, James. You mustn't presume on my friendship with Anne. She trusts me.''

''You're right. I'm sorry.'' He was wearing his little-boy look deliberately now, deliberately and with charm, conveying bewilderment, yet (with his smile) amusement at the bewildered, childlike look.

I turned back to my book and paper-scattered desk. 'A physical point between possibility and reality.' I had been caught between the two of them before. Though usually the contention was over words or actions of less import. We'd be out having Chinese food or a pizza. Anne would catch James eyeing a girl at another table.

''You chauvinist bastard. You never change. Have to check out the tits and ass, eh?''

"Look. Sorry. I wasn't doing that at all. It's a question of aesthetics. An innocent appreciation of beauty."

Each time they would appeal to me — "What do you think?" He'd used the word "girl" instead of "woman", he hadn't vacuumed in two weeks, he'd been seen flirting — yes, flirting with the department secretary.

"Don't ask Sonya," James would protest. "She's the only woman I know who is straight-forward. She doesn't flirt."

"The *only* woman?"

"I've seen you, Anne. So don't pull out your righteous stance again. I've seen you and your smiles."

He fought back, but Anne always managed to retain the morally superior position. Despite his words, he agreed with all her accusations. He was lucky to have her, she unlucky to have him.

I liked Anne, admired her. We all did. She was a master of slogans and abstractions. Each utterance, each word (no matter how worn) that fell from her lips seemed fresh, new. And she was always a step or two ahead of the rest of us on the path of "progressive" thought. She was an artist — just a beginner, of course, just graduated, but already her paintings were attracting attention. And not just from us, her friends, though we were very impressed by this true artist, this person who had been, who was "there", but also from the outside, the establishment. After all, she was young when it paid to be young. She was photogenic: tiny, dark and dramatic. And her art, like her words, had impact — huge, super-realistic paintings of cabbages, artichokes, a cut papaya, intense with minute detail, loud with concept.

A week after the exchange in my office, I was having lunch with Anne in one of those typical late sixties places

— lots of plants and wood, long-haired waiters and veg-
etarian food. This is a story of the sixties though it occured in the early seventies. The old set of laws, the
Newtonian physics of behaviour was seen as limited,
wanting. Experience had shown that they might be ap-
plicable to others (other societies say) but not to "the
free woman" or "the free man" — not to the isolated
self-determined individual that each one of us saw him/
herself as. The new system, the Quantum mechanics of
the person rather than the subatomic particle was no
more than a sketchy set of hypotheses. Unfortunately,
we didn't wait for corroborative data. We treated a ten-
tative, incomplete system as if it were a rigid set of laws,
as if it had no answer, an approach for any eventuality.
We stretched and exaggerated possibilities into slogans
and dogmas: We shall overcome, Never trust anyone
over thirty, The Sexual Revolution, Woman's Libera-
tion, Sisterhood, Truth and not Truth, Illusion and
Reality, Theory and Experience.

That day we were talking of Germaine Greer, Kate
Millett, and Juliet Mitchell, writers we had studied oh-
so-seriously in our Woman's Socialist Education Group.
Though, of course, our tone over the grilled cheese,
avocado and sprout sandwiches was lighter. We digress-
ed. We giggled.

"Don't talk to me of how free you are." Anne was
leaning over her plate, her dark eyes intent. I hadn't
mentioned freedom or myself at all, but I understood
that Anne needed certain devices, certain turns-of-
phrase, to best make her point. "Have you ever tasted
your menstrual blood?"

I stopped chewing. Hot cheese stuck to the top of my
mouth. "Are you kidding?"

"But you have tasted your blood, sucked on a scratch?"

"Of course . . ."

"You see. Don't tell me you have accepted your body, freed yourself from sexist views. Don't tell me." Thick spring dust and stray winter garbage were being blown down the curiously careless street, visible through the window behind Anne, "Admit it." Anne was leaning over the table.

"Well, have you?"

She flipped her thick dark hair back and laughed. "No, I don't find the idea appealing, but Greer is right."

"I don't know. But then I'm a physics teacher. Symbolic gestures don't suit me."

"Gestures? It's more than that, Sonya. Take back your body. Own it. I finally do. After all these years. When I'm with Tom . . ."

"You are still . . . seeing him."

"It's fantastic. Marvellous. Does wonders for the old morale. You should try it. Do you good." Anne crunched emphatically into a carrot stick.

"Try it? Men? I have."

"Throw yourself into a relationship. Throw away caution. Stop looking for meaning. Focus on now, not tomorrow."

"You'd be surprised."

"No, I know you. You're still mooning over Daryl. Six months. You have to go on."

And there, finally, she was right. I had been, was, mooning. Controlled lunacy. Over Daryl who for seven years had been my center, my sun. Mooning, for I had clung to his image, shielded myself with his image through many lonely hours. She was right, though it wasn't until later in the afternoon that I saw it.

We were in one of those little shops, crammed with crumpled Indian cottons, hash pipes, folksy crafts, and incense. Anne was flipping through a rack of dresses while I peered through the dim light at a tray of multi-strand friendship rings. I was amused by Anne's repeated sighs of impatience. She was caught between what she felt she should want to wear, what we believed was correct to wear, and her stronger urge for distinction, for signalling that she was the artist. So the modest long sleeves and earth tones irritated her, but she wasn't ready to scour Eaton's for a backless black satin.

"If only Edmonton had a proper nostalgia store. I'm in the mood for something more . . . costumey." She had almost slipped and said sexy. "Thirties kinds of thing."

"Worn with the proper ironic spirit, of course, a comment on the idea of glamour."

Anne's head lifted at that, her eyes startled. I smiled an I'm-only-teasing smile. But her eyes remained on my face, searching.

I was starting to blush, an obvious burn, an inadvertent declaration. Quickly I turned away, back to the rings. Only to find the best excuse possible for my red cheeks — Daryl. In my distraction I hadn't noticed him entering. Or had I only conjured up the image, my once other half looming in the half light, one hand on the ring tray? Not that I would have ever imagined Daryl looking so embarrassed, still less with that echoing flush.

His hand fell away from the tray. He even took a step forward as if to block my view of the counter. But I already knew that Daryl was no casual browser. He'd found someone and she mattered.

The silence and awkwardness were becoming pointed. Finally he spoke, the polite inquiries of an acquaintance. And I responded in kind. Yet, now and then, his words alluded to the earlier intimacy. "You do look tired. Are you taking your iron pills? Or are you having trouble sleeping again?" And following the earlier pattern, I smiled and bristled.

"The observed system cannot be observed until it interacts with the observing system."

Anne's hand was on my arm. "You'll be late for class."

"*Class.* You have to go." She was actually pulling me out of the store.

"Good thing I was with you. You kept *staring* at him."

Moonstruck. "It was the shock."

"I had to drag you out." Our eyes met and this time there was recognition, kinship. I began to giggle. We laughed, snorted, sprawled over the red vinyl booths of the tacky coffee shop she'd steered me into. "MEN."

"An hour ago you were prescribing them for me."

"I was suggesting another type of situation."

"Can we control the type of situation? Life isn't a laboratory experiment."

Anne pushed her hair behind her ears, exposing her pale oval face. "You have to avoid the old roles. That's where we're straightjacketed. You should have seen yourself. Little Miss Submissive. Yes Daryl. No Daryl. Little Miss Take Care of Me. I've become obsessed with the roles women play — need to play; I want to use it in my art." Her chin was jutting out, her fingers in her hair, twining, pulling as quick and compulsive as her words. "I'm thinking of abandoning painting. I'd like to use fabric, weaving, needlework maybe — traditional

female mediums — use them in sculptural forms. Angora
wool and glass shards. Can you see it? Use them to comment. A wife. The other woman. Representations of the
old, old cliches. Those male concepts that imprison us
. . . I know. Married to James, how can I not know?''
Her face was twisting ever so slightly, her mouth curling. ''I've had it with him and all his fluffy little bon-
bons. Woman as object. Woman as cute little package.
I see him looking. Every damn time.''

''Don't say that . . . I'm sure they don't mean anything to him. After all you have hardly been the traditional faithful wife. You are so important to him.''

''We agreed to be free. We agreed to enjoy others.
To experiment. But nothing serious. No real involve-
ments. Now he's serious.''

''No.''

''What's wrong with you? I know.'' Her voice was
beginning to break, her eyes to glass over. She was
oblivious to the two women in the next booth, oblivious
to the cup of cold coffee, oblivious to what I knew must
be showing on my face.

''You think he has someone?''

''He hasn't touched me in two months.''

Two months. The sun had poured through the open
curtains, coating the twisted, flowered sheets. Sweet
honey sun, highlighting James's lean pale body, catching
the hidden gold in his hair. Light, a particle. Dust danced
in the shafts of sunshine. My body against his was sharply
there, sharply alive. Light, a wave. Our coming together
had carried me, transported me; I had flowed to another
place, briefly become another me. Flesh made light. Flesh
made energy.

Two months. Yet, the afternoon after my conversation

with Anne, lying in his arms, I could not ask him. My experience and my words were in two separate compartments. The new rules insisted such transports need nothing more than recreation, a healthy exercise. And James had always spoken of our afternoons in that tone. He had insisted at the beginning that he would be open and honest with me. He needed a little diversion and I obviously needed to get over Daryl. A bit of fun would be therapeutic for me. He'd gone as far as using the words 'just what the doctor ordered.' Having accepted his words and tone I could not now ask, what do your touches mean? What does *this,* this joy mean? And what does that which is between you and Anne mean?

I ran my hand over his chest and he posed a question. "Have I replaced Daryl?" His eyes, through the smoke of his cigarette, had their habitual piercing expression. He and Anne had matching intensities, matching glittering eyes.

"Of course not." Could one person ever replace another? I had clutched at Daryl's image for so long. "What's between us is different." But what was between us? Confusion, the collision of random bodies? "This —" I was up on one elbow and used the other arm to gesture, waving it to encompass the bed, "is *very* nice."

He laughed and pulled me back down to him. "Very nice . . ." Graphically he complimented my abilities, my style. I was foolishly flattered, amused that, with my limited experience, he rated me at the top of the three dozen or so women he claimed to have known. "Excluding Anne, of course. But an objective evaluation."

It was only later, remembering, that I realized how we avoided coping with the actual experience of each other. And only later still, that I hadn't avoided the truth,

I just didn't know it. I still don't. I know only the *potentia,* that place between the idea and the actual.

A week after that last afternoon with James, Anne phoned. She was crying. She and James had had a fight. No worse than usual. But when she'd returned from the studio, he was gone. There was a note that announced he was "mixed up." Since the term was over, his marks were in, he was taking time "for himself."

I never expected the pain I felt, a deep physical maiming. I wasn't supposed to feel such loss. My wonder, a wonder that has stretched over all these years, at that surprising, illicit pain is at the centre of this story. A story of the sixties. Now, the dogmas have shrunk back to possibilities, the slogans have developed subordinate clauses and modifiers. Now, we don't forget that the new laws are not yet maximal. But, we cannot return to the fifities, to the old narrow straight-forward laws. Light, a particle. Light, a wave. Yet it cannot be both wave and particle. Einstein's and Bohr's question remains "is our theory too poor or our experience too rich?"

James had taken a summer job up north with a surveying crew. I could see him, his small-boy round head, his dark eyes, sitting with the other men around a campfire each long, pale evening. He would sing, his voice was poor, but he loved to pick at his guitar. He would talk, encouraging others to recount their stories, 'to shape their personal histories.' "Tell me," he'd say. Or "Let me tell you — women . . ." And sometimes, when it was very late, he would indulge his pedantic side and lecture a bit about probabilities and reality, waves and particles, all the quirks and quarks, safe in the male world, out of reach of both of us.

Sandra Birdsell

FALLING IN LOVE

I get off the bus and I stand beside the highway at
Jordon Siding, wondering what to do now. I've come
to a dead end. Stopped by the reality of a churned-up
landscape. For shitsake, as Larry, the past-love-of-my-
life, would say. Today, in late June, while the fields
around me are growing towards harvest, I am empty.
I'm split in two. One part of me can think, what are
you going to do? And the other is off somewhere,
wandering through empty rooms, bumping into dusty
furniture, hoping that this may be a dream. And that
Larry is still here.

"I'm sorry you didn't know — ah," the bus driver
searches for the correct word. Am I Miss or Ma'am?
he pushes his cap back on his chunky sandy head and
glances down and then away from my breasts which

nudge out against Larrry's denim shirt. No, I'm not wearing a bra. His glance is at once shifty and closed as though he is guilty of betraying me, too. And immediately, I'm glad that at least I have not made the mistake of being pregnant. Grateful that I never gave in to those odd flashes of desire to make love without a contraceptive, to play a kind of roulette game with sex.

"Didn't they tell you when you bought the ticket that the road was under construction?" the bus driver asks. His eyes take in the shoebox I carry beneath my arm, tied closed with butcher string, air holes punched in it so Satan can breathe. A going-away present from Larry, a black rabbit. He has taken off, Larry has, has flown the coop and left me with the rabbit and one measly shirt to remind me of him. Larry, I'm remembering you in the briny smell of armpits.

I remember this morning, the acne-faced girl in the coffee shop at the bus depot in Manitou saying something about having to go to Winnipeg and then back south to get to Agassiz. But my mind wasn't paying attention. I was aware instead of her squinty mean eyes enjoying the lapsed state of my affair. Larry Cooper is wild, I'd been warned, and he's lazier than a pet coon. And I told myself that they were just jealous. There are no calipers wide enough to measure the scoured sides of my stupidity. This year, I have learned something about the eternal combustion engine, about love.

Before me, where I should be making my connection with another Grey Goose bus that will carry me thirty miles east across farming country to Agassiz and back into the bosom of my family, the road is a muddy upheaval of rocks, slippery clay and topsoil. Under destruction. The whole world is under destruction. Larry

used the word 'dead-end.' And so he has turned the other
way, headed down the highway to Montreal to work in
his brother-in-law's car rental business.

"If you love someone, let him go," Larry's mother
said. "And if he comes back, he's yours. Whatever you
do, don't take this thing personal, okay? Larry's like that.
Every spring, he takes off. Spring fever, it's in his
blood," she said. And then she evicted me.

"You'd better get back on the bus and make your connection in Winnipeg," the driver says and it's clear from
his tone that he's decided I'm a Miss which gives him
certain authority. I'm aware of faces in the windows looking out at me, slight bemusement with my predicament.
I see in the window my greasy black hair tied up into
a pony tail, Larry's shirt, my jeans held at the waist with
safety pins because I have lost ten pounds. My luggage
is an Eaton's shopping bag.

When I woke up and discovered Larry missing, I
didn't worry at first because he often went out riding
before dawn. He liked to be alone in the early morning. Larry liked to watch the sun rise. "He's out ripping off truck parts, you mean," his mother said, rais-
ing an artfully plucked eyebrow and flicking cigarette
ashes into her coffee cup. But she didn't know Larry the
way I thought I did. He would come back to me, crawl
beneath the sheets, hairy limbs still cool from the early
morning air, breath minty and sweet, and he would wind
himself around me and describe the colour of the sun
on a barn roof, or the distinct pointed clatter of a tractor starting up. On such a morning, he brought Satan
to me because he said its shiny black coat, its constant
nibbling, reminded him of me. On such a morning, he
came home and invented a gadget that cooked weiners

electrically. He stuck wires into each end of the weiner, plugged it into the wall and instantly, cooked weiner. Another morning, he was inspired to try to build a more effective water pump.

I lay in bed waiting for Larry, looking up at the new ceiling tiles overhead. His mother let us live rent-free in those three rooms above the butcher shop if we fixed the caved-in ceiling. I liked the suite the way it was when we first moved in, sawdust and shavings ankle deep on the floor, ceiling slats dangling free, the lone lightbulb suspended by a single twined wire. It was early Canadian Catastrophe. It reminded me that when I met Larry, I was sitting in the hotel cafe in Agassiz, between jobs, waiting for the world to end. For a year, I'd had the feeling that a bomb was going to drop and that would be the end of us all. For this reason, I left school. I was filling in time, waiting, and then Larry walked in and I thought that if the bomb fell that day, I'd rather be dead with him than anyone else.

But Larry wouldn't live with a caved-in ceiling and when he'd fixed that, he enamelled the kitchen counters black. And the paint never quite dried and if we let a dish stand on it overnight, it became permanently stuck there. And then I went crazy and hand-stitched curtains for the windows in the front room. Larry nailed Christmas-tree lights onto the wall above the couch and we made love in their multi-coloured glow. We made love every single day for six months.

I waited for Larry to return and listened at the same time to the rats thumping about in the butcher shop below, dragging bones from the bone box. (I never minded the rats, I figured they worked hard for what they got.) Above me, near the ceiling, a shaft of light came through the small window, spotlighting Larry's note taped to the closet door. I knew before reading it that Larry had left me. I have this built-in premonition for bad news. As I reached for the note, I could smell Larry, like alkali, dry, metallic, in the palms of my hands. And scattered in the sheets were his c-shaped blond pubic hairs. I read the note and became extremely tired, as though a thick black woollen hood had suddenly fallen into place over my head.

Two days later, Larry's mother dropped by. She told me to get out of bed. She wanted her sheets back. She had me clean out the fridge. I brought along the left-overs of our relationship in the shopping bag. Lettuce for Satan, a dimpled, wilted grapefruit and one beer. And resentment, which is a thick sludge clogging my chest. If Larry, by some miracle, showed up now, I would jump on his skinny back, grab hold of his blond hair and wrestle him to the ground. I would stomp on his adam's apple.

"Forget it," I say to the bus driver. "I'm not going all the way to Winnipeg. Just forget it."

He laughs. "I don't see what choice you have." He puts his sunglasses back on and I can see myself in them. And it seems to me that he, along with everyone else, conspires against me. That I have never had a choice. "You looked at my ticket when I got on. Why didn't you say something?"

"I thought you knew."

I pick up the shopping bag and begin to walk away. "Well, I didn't. And I'm not spending three bloody hours on the bus. So, I guess I'll walk."

He blocks my way. "Whoa. Agassiz is thirty miles away. And it's going to be one hot day." He scans the cloudless sky.

Larry, you creep. This is all your fault. "What's it
to you whether I walk or ride?"

The driver's thick neck flares red. He steps aside.
"Right. It's no skin off my nose. If you want to walk
thirty miles in the blazing sun, go ahead. It's a free
country."

The bus roars down the highway, leaving me in a
billow of hot sharp-smelling smoke. The sound of the
engine grows fainter and then I'm alone, facing that
churned-up muddy road where no vehicle could ever
pass. Thirty bloody miles. God-damn you, Larry. I hear
a meadowlark trilling and then a squealing rhythmic
sound of metal on metal. It comes from a BA gas sign
swinging back and forth above two rusting gas bowsers
that stand in front of a dilapidated wood-frame building.
Jordon Siding garage and store. Eureka. A telephone.
I will call home and say, guess what? No, I'll say, it's
your prodigal daughter, to get them thinking along
charitable lines. I have seen the light. But all that is
another issue, one I don't have the energy to think about.
Plants fill the dusty store window and off to one side,
in a tiny yard, freshly laundered clothes flutter from a
clothesline.

I enter the dim interior and feel surrounded. The at-
mosphere is dreary, relentlessly claustrophobic. It's a
typical country store and yet it reminds me of old things,
of fly-specked calendars, lambs and young girls in straw
hats, smiling with cherry-painted lips, innocent smiles.
And me pulling a toboggan through the streets of Agassiz
each New Year, collecting calendars, trekking through
the fragile blue sphere of a winter night that seemed to
embrace all ages so that as I bumped along ice and snow,
I thought, years ago someone like me was doing this,

may still be doing this. But at the same time, I felt the
world dangling like a bauble about to shatter on the floor.
I went to the garages, grocery stores, the bank. I needed many calendars because during the year each time
a month ended, I wrote messages on the backs of the
spent time and hid the messages in the garden, in flower
pots, beneath stones, for people from another world to
discover when I would be gone. A fly buzzes suddenly
against the window, trapped between the foliage of the
plants and the glass. Beyond, a counter, glass casing,
but there's nothing inside it but shelf-lining, old
newspapers.

"Hello, anyone here?" I call in the direction of the
backrooms behind the varnished counter where I imagine
potatoes boil in a pot, a child sleeps on a blanket on the
floor while its mother ignores my voice, sits in an over-
stuffed chair (the type Larry and I inherited with our
suite, an olive green, scratchy velour couch and chair),
reading a magazine. What is she reading, I wonder? I
look about me. No telephone in sight.

Outside once again, I face that bleak turned-up landscape and begin walking in the direction of Agassiz. I
face the sun and walk off to the side of the road, following the deep imprint left behind by one of the monstrous
yellow machines that sits idle in the field beyond. Why
aren't there any men on the machines? Why aren't they
working today? I begin to feel uneasy. The sounds of
the countryside rise up and Satan thumps violently
against his box in answer. Around me stretch broad fields
dotted with clumps of trees. In the distance a neat row
of trees, planted as a windbreak, shades a small farmhouse and outbuildings. Overhead, the flat cloudless sky,
no perspective, I cannot gauge distance. It's as though

this is a calendar picture of a landscape and I have
somehow entered into it. Except for yellow grasshoppers
sprinting up before my feet and the tireless hovering of
flies above the ditches, there is no movement anywhere.
I turn around. The garage is still the same distance. I
can turn back and wait for a car and hitch a ride to Winnipeg. I could go back to Manitou. But it seems to me
that I have been set in this direction, that it's inevitable.
I walk for an hour. Satan continues to struggle. I stop
to rest, lift the lid off the box a crack and push wilted
lettuce through to him. I sit down, take Larry's note from
my shirt pocket and unfold it on my knee.

Dear Lureen,

*I'm sorry if you got your hopes up. Like the song goes, you
always hurt the one you love, the one you shouldn't hurt at all.
That's life. But this town is a dead-end. You know what I mean.
I think I'll take my sister up on her offer.*

*You are okay. Don't think I'm leaving because of you. I know
you will get over me. Anyway, if it works out, I'll send you
some money. I might send you enough to come to Montreal. I'll
see. It just depends.*

*You can have Satan. I don't trust my mother to look after him
anyway. Once she forgot to feed my goldfish and they all turned
belly-up. Notice, I am leaving you my denim shirt because you
liked it so much.*

Tell the old lady not to get in a sweat.

Luv U,
Larry.

"Whatever you do," Larry's mother said when he
introduced us, "don't get married." A cigarette dangled
from one corner of her mouth and she squinted hard at

me through the blue smoke. She was blonde, like Larry, and I thought that at one time she must have been beautiful, you could see flashes of it sometimes when she wasn't being sarcastic. "I'm only telling you for your own good," she said later when Larry was out of the room. "He's like his father. Lazier than a pet coon."

Larry was not lazy. He could pull the head off a motor, ream out the cylinders, do a ring and valve job in two days flat. I'd tell him I wanted to go to the dance at Rock Lake and he'd rebuild the transmission that afternoon so we could go. He opened the housing, called me down the stairs to come and see the giant cogs, how the gears were supposed to mesh. And I couldn't help but think the combustion engine is a joke, or at least a hoax perpetrated on man to keep him busy tinkering so he can't think about what's really happening. Wheels moving wheels, moving pulleys, moving more metal and so much motion for so little effect, arms, lifters, valves, wheezing breathers, springs, filters, cylinders, shoes, things pressing against other things, grinding, particles of chewed-up metal sifting into other important parts. God, it was overwhelming. Faulty timing, a coughing, farting engine, a rotten swaying front end, screeching wheelbearings, all these problems Larry and I faced and overcame in six months.

"Okay Larry," I said, wanting to say, this is silly. "There has got to be a much simpler way than the eternal combustion engine."

"Internal, internal combustion engine," he said, "and anyway, you are paid not to think, but to do." So, okay, I played the game. I soaked bolts and other metal shapes in my dishpan, brushed them down with Varsol, removed grease with a paring knife, had them looking like new. I learned how to install brushes in a generator. I took it apart in my lap. I thought the copper wires were beautiful. And then, that what I was doing was important. That maybe I'd like to have a part in the running of the internal combustion machine. And the next time Larry complained about having to wash his feet with his socks on, maybe I'd let him ride bareback for awhile. Maybe the two of us could open a garage?

Larry flicked the end of my nose with a greasy finger and said no way would he put in four years getting his papers just to satisfy some government-hired jerk who had never taken apart anything more complicated than a Zippo lighter.

And always, we made it to the dance on time. That night, we'd be cruising down the highway, eating up the miles to Rock Lake, radio turned up full volume, Larry driving with two fingers and reaching with his other hand for me, naked beneath my sundress. And the gears would be meshing and the motor singing, the timing tuned just right and the radio playing all our favourite hits. And Larry would squeeze my breast and say, hey, honey bunch. Remind me to slow down long before we get to the corner, okay? I got no brakes.

Ancient history. Ancient bloody history. I rest my head against my knees and I don't want to cry, Larry's not worth it, but I do. And then I take the lid off the shoebox and I pet Satan for a few moments and then I carry him to the side of the road and drop him into the tall grass. He scurries away without a backward glance.

"Do you think it's true," Larry said, turning away from me to examine his naked physique in the mirror, "that a large ass means a short sex life? That's what my mother told me."

And I spent the next two hours convincing him that she was wrong and that he had the neatest, hardest, turned-in buttocks I had ever seen. Bullshit. I wish for Larry an extremely short sex life. May he never have sex again. I pick up the shopping bag, swing it back and forth a couple of times and let loose. It flies across the ditch and whacks against the telephone pole. Screw yourself, Larry. Stick your scrawny dink in your ear.

Free now, I walk faster, arms swinging, following the fish-bone tire pattern pressed into the yellow clay. I will go to Winnipeg, look for work. Or I will go to bed and stay there. Or I could go back to school.. And then I hear a sound, the sound of a motor geared down low — Larry? My heart leaps. I wouldn't put it past him. Larry can do anything. Even materialize out of thin air. I look up. There on the crest of the muddy graded mound is a pale blue car, the bullet-nosed shape of a 51 Studebaker. It slithers sideways, first one way and then the other. It stops, starts, makes its way slowly towards me. I see a man behind the wheel, copper red hair, a brushcut. Not Larry. The car comes to a stop and the man opens the door. I measure the distance to the farmhouse beyond. Could I outrun him? He unfolds from the seat. He's match-like, tall and thin. He stands up, shakes creases from his grey slacks, tiptoes across the ruts in shiny brown penny loafers and I begin to relax. He looks harmless.

He stretches out a long pale hand to me. It looks fragile, like worn porcelain. I keep my hands behind my back. He doesn't seem to mind and folds his, one over-top the other across his stomach. He tilts back slightly on his heels and smiles down at me. "Well, well. Bless you. This is the day that the Lord hath made. Let's just

take a moment to rejoice in it.'' He breathes deeply.
''Thank you Jesus.''

God. A pentecostal fanatic. One of the holy rollers.

''I saw you coming down from the corner and I said
to myself, 'now there's the reason God had for waking
you up this morning.'' He lifts his hand suddenly, pokes
a long finger into his red hair and scratches.

A grasshopper leaps up between us and lands on the
roof of the car. I can see a resemblance between the in-
sect and the man, long limbs, angles, ball-bearing shaped
eyes.

''So you're stranded then,'' he says.

''I didn't know about this.'' I indicate the up-turned
road.

''No matter,'' he says. He flutters his flimsy hands
in my direction and catches himself on the chin in the
process. I begin to like him. His smile is wide, lights up
his steel grey eyes. ''Everything works out for the good
in the end. For those that trust in Him. Where are you
hoping to get to?''

Life, I want to say. I am hoping to get through life
but I don't think I will. ''Agassiz.''

''Agassiz. Well, well. The heavenly Father has given
me business just outside of Agassiz. I can get you close
to it. Closer than this. Didn't I say everything would
work out?''

He leads the way around to the passenger side, opens
the door and suddenly I feel awkward. Larry would let
me crawl through the window before he'd think to open
a door for me. The car is like new inside. The seats are
covered in clear plastic. A sheet of plastic lies on the floor.
On the dash is what looks to be a deck of playing cards
but the box says, ''Thought For Today.'' Clipped to

the sun visor is another card that reads, "I am a Flying Farmer."

He turns the car around in stages and soon we are bumping down the road, mud scraping against the bottom of the car. Despite the good condition of the car, there's a slight ticking and I want to tell him that he ought to watch the valves but I don't think it would be polite. I look over my shoulder and sure enough, tell-tale blue smoke billows from the exhaust. He's a clumsy driver, shifts gears too soon, strains the engine, rides the clutch. And then the tires grab hold of a groove of deep ruts and he speeds up, letting the car find its own path.

"So, what's your story?" he asks after awhile.

"Story?"

"Sure. The Lord sends me lots of people. I know when someone has a story."

And so I begin the way I always do, with the question that makes people frown or shrug or walk away. "Have you ever thought that at this very moment someone may be pressing a button and the world may come to an end? And we'll all be instant cooked weiners?"

He laughs. "Now why would I want to waste my time thinking about that? I couldn't live with those negative thoughts hanging over my head all the time. I know that He is able to keep me against that day. Whatever a man thinks, that's what he is. And I think about all the good things we've got." He thumps the wheel for emphasis, sticks his head out the window. "Look around you, this country is beaudyfull. Good crops this year. The fields are white unto the harvest. Thank you Jesus." He begins to hum to himself as we slither down the road. Then he sucks something loose from his teeth. "Cooked weiners, my, my. That just won't happen. Know how

I know? Because I wouldn't be here right now if that was true. The Lord would have returned already if it was the end of the world and I wouldn't be here. I'd be with Him.''

I know the story. I have been brought up on this. Graves opened, the rapture of the saints. People reaching towards a shining light. Whenever I heard the story, I would imagine grabbing hold of a tree on the way up so I could stay behind. ''How do you know that's true?''

He laughs once again. ''And how do you know that it isn't? It takes more faith to believe that it isn't true than to believe that it is. Know why? Because of hope. Man is born with hope right in him and you've got to go against the grain not to believe. Now tell me, what's the story behind the story? What brings you here today, to this place, this time?''

And suddenly, my tongue takes off and I tell him everything, about being young and hiding pieces of paper from the calendar that say, 'Whoever finds this, my name was Lureen Lafreniere, I lived in Agassiz, Manitoba. This month when I was running, I slipped and fell and cut my hand on a sharp piece of ice. Five stitches.'

''For awhile, I stopped doing this, I thought it was a silly thing to do. But it came back to me, the feeling, so strong, that I couldn't sit still in school. I had to get up and move, just do something, because I felt that something terrible was going to happen that would prevent me from . . . from . . .''

''From doing all the things you want to do even though you aren't even sure what it is you want to do.''

''Yes.''

''There's nothing new under the sun. I've heard that one before.''

"Yes, but just when man says, nothing is new, every-thing is the same as yesterday, then comes the end. Therefore, watch and wait."

He smiles and his smile makes me smile. "You know your scripture. Bless you sister."

And then I tell him how I met Larry, about the past six months, about the feeling of impending doom leav-ing me. I talk to him as though I have known him for years and he doesn't ever interrupt, just says "whoops" and "bless you" when we hit large clumps of mud. I talk non-stop, as though this man were sent for just this reason. And when I finish, he doesn't answer for a long time, just squints near-sightedly at the road and I think that I have made a mistake. I hold my breath and wait for his sermon. The Thou Shalt Nots.

"You love him," he says finally and puts a long, slender, cool hand over mine.

"Yeah," I realize this is true. That I am in love with Larry. While waiting for the world to end, I have fallen in love. I fell for Larry Cooper. I'm falling.

"Well, well. Love is great. Love is wonderful. The Lord knew what He was doing when He created Adam and Eve."

I wipe my eyes on Larry's denim shirt.

"That fella of yours will come back. You can be sure of that."

"He will?"

He squeezes my hand. "Believe it and it will happen. Tell yourself, Larry's coming back."

Shit. The power of positive thinking crap. "Larry's pretty stubborn, you don't know him like I do."

"Shh. I understand, you know Larry and you may be right. But that's only one side of it. Listen, this is my story. Long time ago, I was in a bad accident. A plane crash. I went down in the bush in northern Manitoba. I thought I was finished. I walked in circles for two days with a broken collarbone. When I came upon the plane the second time, I cried. Broke right down. And then a verse from the Bible came to me. It was, 'Not by might, nor by power, but by my spirit.' It was the Lord telling me to trust Him. So I knelt in the bush and I prayed and I said, 'Okay God. I'm lost. I can't find the way myself. I've already tried. And I'm tired and I'm injured and so I have no choice. I'm going to trust you. Show me the way.' And I opened my eyes, got up, started walking and I hadn't walked more than five minutes and there in front of me was a road. A paved road. So you see, from my side of it, I was finished. There was nothing I could do. But from God's side, He had only just begun. And God knows Larry better than you do.''

I want to say, I know how that happened. Often, when you try too hard, the answer escapes you. You have to give up and then the inner mind brings the answer to the surface. There wasn't anything supernatural about your experience. It happens all the time. I bite my tongue.

''That's very nice,'' I say.

He turns to me in astonishment. ''Nice? I tell you about my wonderful experience, how the Lord delivered me and you say, 'that's nice'? It was more than nice, sister. It was a frigging miracle.''

Would an angel swear? I ponder the question later that evening as I lie in bed in the front bedroom of my house in Agassiz. He dropped me off three miles from town, near the elevators, and when I turned to tell him,

as a favour, that he'd better get the valves checked, the
car had vanished. I was shocked. And I sat down beside
the road to think about it. I rubbed my stiff calf muscles,
my feet burned as though I had walked a great distance.
And I came to the conclusion that I had imagined meeting that man. The mind can do that. It was a way of
coping with the situation I was in. But the question in-
trigues me. Would an angel swear? And was that swearing? I have always imagined swearing to mean to swear
on something, to have to prove in some way the fact that
you are telling the truth. The error of not being
trustworthy.

The reception I received from my family was surprising. My mother was strangely tender, as though I had
fallen ill with a fever. My younger brothers and sisters
regarded me as someone who had come from a long way
away, a distant relative, and they were guarded and shy.
"Are you expecting?" my mother asked while the two
of us changed the linen on the bed in the front bedroom.
And I said, "No. But I wish I was." She flicked the sheet
and smoothed it straight. "No you don't," she said.
"You just think you do, but you really don't."

As I lie in bed, the sounds around me are all familiar.
The town siren blares out the ten o'clock curfew. The
curtains on the window are the same ones I've had since
I can remember. But I pull the sheet up around me and
I feel like a guest, a visitor in the home I grew up in.
How will I ever be able to sleep without Larry?

I remember our first date. Larry showing off, climb-
ing up on a snowplow in the municipal yards, starting
it, and ripping through the chainlink fence before he
could figure out how to stop it. And later, driving eighty
miles to crawl across the roof of the butcher shop, break-

ing a window to get into the suite and still wearing our parkas; it was bitterly cold, I gave up my virginity while our breath hung in clouds of frost in the air above us and the beer we'd bought popped the caps and climbed up in frosty towers from the bottles. Afterward, teeth chattering, we chewed frozen malt and Larry warmed my hands in his armpits.

The memory climbs up the back of my throat, finds its way into my eyes, leaks down the sides of my face into the pillow. Okay, God. I'll give you this one chance. This miracle involves another person, his own stubborn will. I clench my teeth. I feel as though I am levitating off the bed. This is it. Thanks for bringing Larry back to me.

I sigh. I'm calm. Tension seeps from me as I lie in the room where I have first thought of love and making it happen. And I hear the breeze in the trees outside the window. I have hidden many particles of time beneath its branches. I see the faint glow of the town. And if I got up, I would see the green watertower and the siren on it that orders the movement of my town. I would see the skating rink, and my father coming down from the corner on his way home from the Hotel to the news that Lureen's back. And then I hear it, a jangle of keys that stiffens my spine, sends my heart jumping. Then a cough. I'm rigid, listening. A whistle. I leap down the bed, pull aside the curtains and I see him below, his narrow pale face turned up to the window, Larry in his white windbreaker, collar turned up, the glow of his cigarette.

"Larry?"

"For shitsake. What's keeping you?" he asks.

And I run barefoot down the stairs, through the rooms, out the front door and then Larry catches me

by the wrist and pulls me to him, wraps me around his
skinny shivering body.

"Blew a rod at Thunder Bay," he says. "I couldn't
fix it."

Liar. "I'm sorry," I say. He kisses me. His mouth
is chilly and warm at the same time. I wedge my tongue
between his shivering lips.

He pulls away. "I caught a ride with a real weirdo.
He offered me fifty bucks if I'd jerk him off. So I said
to hell with it and I took the first bus going west."

"Hey, honey bunch," I whisper into his neck, "Let's
go to the park. We can talk tomorrow."

"The park, what for?" But I can feel him growing
hard against my stomach. "I haven't got anything on
me. You know." His tongue answers mine and it's like
the faint fluttering of a moth.

I link my arm through his and lead him in the direction I want to go. "Oh, by the way, I let Satan loose."

He stops walking, frowns. "What did you go and do
that for?"

"Well, he was heavy, Larry. I suppose you never
thought of that. And there I was, thirty miles from
nowhere. I had to walk because the bloody road was
under construction, so what was I supposed to do?"

"You've got all the brains," Larry says. "Why ask
me?"

And we walk arm and arm down the road, Larry and
me going to the park.

Lois Simmie

THE NIGHT WATCHMAN

> *I am like a pelican of the wilderness:*
> *I am like an owl of the desert.*
>
> *For I have eaten ashes like bread,*
> *and mingled my drink with weeping*
>
> *Psalm 102:6, 9*

They came on a hot summer morning just as the
Children's Parade slowly wound its way along College
Drive and down the Twenty-fifth Street Bridge. In the
clear, windy sky, high above the snapping flags, the noise
and glitter of the parade, they came — wave after wave
of enormous white birds, like a squadron of bombers
sweeping toward the bridge.

"Cranes!" someone shouted. "Whooping cranes!"

Matthew looked up, and something caught at his heart.

"Geese!" someone else called. "No, cranes!" another. But they couldn't be cranes. There were too many of them.

The parade became confused, disorderly, a forest of arms pointing up as more and more of the huge birds soared over the bridge, the sun caught in their snowy white bodies, their immense, black-bordered wings.

Shriners, resplendent in red, green and gold, were poised at the top of the bridge. From tiny motorcycles, shiny red convertibles, wooden hobby horses, they looked up. Behind them on the parade route that wound up past the university campus, a gigantic Orphan Annie stared round-eyed across the river, her arm around her faithful dog Sandy. Beyond the Annie float, the Bonnie Bluebells in sweltering plaid gamely marched in place, flushed cheeks bulging. Droning bars of "Amazing Grace" carried faintly to the bridge.

On the bridge, the Sesame Street float was stalled. Big Bird had stopped dead, his yellow feathers plastered to his skinny frame, and his bill pointing skyward. Count Dracula stopped counting and stared up, his black cape billowing around his small, white face, as the last of the birds passed over the bridge. Above Rotary Park, their reconnaissance flight complete, they banked into the wind, spiralling higher and higher till the sky was filled with brilliant white flight, then streamed back towards the bridge in a long, straight line.

"Pelicans," said a voice, filled with wonder. "They're pelicans." And Matthew Winter realized that the voice was his.

The parade was forgotten as everyone stared up. "Seventeen, eighteen, nineteen, twenty," shouted the Count, who had recovered enough to seize the opportunity. The birds flew lower on their way back, each pair of outspread wings spanning at least seven feet. "Twenty-five, twenty-six, twenty-seven . . ." Matthew heard the wind in their feathers, and noted with amusement the relaxed S-shape of head and neck in flight, which gave the huge birds a droll, "just along for the ride" look. As the last one flew over, Matthew was working his way through the crowd to the side of the bridge for an unobstructed view of their departure.

Downriver, past where the glistening water slid over the dam, was a narrow green island dotted with gulls. As the strains of "Amazing Grace" grew louder, the pelicans skimmed toward the island, losing altitude like planes approaching an aircraft carrier, and one by one they braked and landed, turning the island into a magical summer snowdrift.

As the last float rolled past the end of the bridge, Matthew veered to the right, escaping the crowd, and headed along the river bank toward the snowdrift. Chunks of it were breaking off and floating out into the water, and when Matthew reached the place where the river spilled, smooth and shining, over the dam, the big birds were forming a long line there to feed. Stationing themselves a few feet apart and about the same distance back from the dam, they patiently waited for the churning water to serve up fish.

One pelican fished far from the rest and near the cement apron where Matthew stood. Close enough for him to see the water sluicing from its long orange bill, see fish disappear inside the veiny, flesh-colored pouch.

Close enough to observe what a queer, unlovely creature it was when not in flight. It was odd, their coming this late in the summer. Something must have gone wrong at the nesting ground.

Gulls wheeled excitedly over the pelicans, "klee-aah klee-aah klee-ah"'s mingling with the crashing of water over the dam. Matthew smiled as he sat down to watch.

Matthew Winter was a solitary man. He worked alone, walked alone, slept alone, and sometimes, when something seen or remembered made the need to be touched too insistent, he would quiet it himself, feeling, afterward, more desolate than ever.

Matthew once had a wife, but she had left years ago. Because of his drinking, she said. Because he was ugly and unlovable, he heard. Clothing hung on his tall frame like a suit on a rack, and his big ears stood almost at right angles to his head. His nose was large and squashy, the kind of nose a child might fashion from plasticene. Matthew suffered still, at fifty-six, from a stomach-knotting shyness he'd never been able to overcome.

Alcohol had eased it for years until, like a skillful thief who takes only small change at first, it gradually robbed him of everything. His deadly earnest attempt to kill himself — he'd failed even at that — had brought him in a screeching ambulance from his rooming house to the hospital. To a room where hypos grew striped hides, malevolent eyes, flicking tongues; where a man in a blue coverall vacuumed the shining hallway with a large python; and where once, horrifyingly, an orderly pulled a newborn snake from its nest in a cigarette case, placed it between his lips, and set fire to it with a gold lighter.

"Murderer!" Matthew had screamed, as everything slid out of control once again.

"Murderer!" as they folded him inside a straight jacket one more time.

"Crazy old coot," said the orderly to the nurse. He puffed on the snake, which sizzled in a ghastly way.

"Crazy as a shithouse rat," said the orderly, whisking out of the room.

And all night long, sopping wet rats in straight jackets walked up out of the toilet and around the room, leaving damp little tracks and puddles everywhere. Matthew laughed till he hurt at the paranoid expressions on their little rat faces. That was the night he stopped screaming and started getting better.

From the hospital, he went to a treatment centre, and then, at his psychiatrist's recommendation, to a halfway house for recovering alcoholics. He'd been at Hope Haven a month now.

Living with fourteen other people had not eased his sense of isolation. The empty space inside him was not made smaller by the way the light fell on the plastic furniture, by footsteps sighing down the hall to the cigarette-stained bathroom, by the slap slap slap of cards at four in the morning. He was uneasy with the too-fast friendships, the souls laid bare under the awful light, the chipped cups.

But most of all he was distressed by the aura of failed past that weighted the air in the rooms, shadowed the corners. Even the term, halfway house, made him ill at ease. He didn't know where he was halfway to, or from, and couldn't bring himself to care. Soon he would move, he kept telling himself. But somehow he didn't.

The parade was a topic of conversation as they sat around the big kitchen table that evening. Supper had been especially bad because Ruby, the cook, had met her estranged husband that afternoon to talk about a divorce. At first Matthew thought Ruby was a widow, because she always dressed completely in black, and she cried as she stirred things, her black pockets bulging with lumpy, wet kleenex. The food reflected Ruby's emotional state. Soggy, tasteless casseroles, cakes that slumped tiredly in upon themselves.

"Yessir, a lot of work goes into those parades," Wilf said. "I'll never forget seeing the Rose Bowl parade in '62. Right out of this world, man."

"Was everything made of roses?" asked Ruby, from her stool by the stove, where she sat smoking a cigarette and dropping ashes in the pan under the electric burner.

"Everything but the people," Wilf said. "Well, maybe not all roses, but flowers. Every damn thing made of flowers."

"I don't believe that," said Rafe, in his flat, un-equivocal voice. Rafe was Cree, about twenty years old, with long black hair held back in a ponytail. He was a determined loner, who appeared to find Wilf's cheerful babble especially irritating.

"That's your privilege, man," Wilf said, going on to describe the wonders of the Rose Bowl.

The kitchen didn't depress Matthew like the rest of the house. The light was different there, the walls a soft yellow, probably the only room where the paint hadn't been donated by a paint store at inventory time. Some vestiges of the gracious home it had once been still re-mained, in the leaded glass panels in the front door and upstairs hallway, the oak doors and heavy glass door-knobs.

"I liked the Cinderella float best today," said Verla,

the beautiful seventeen-year-old with the most perfect teeth Matthew had ever seen. "I loved the ugly sisters."

"Yeah, I thought one of 'em looked a lot like you, Verla." Wilf grinned at her and then around the table. With his soft, brown beard and little, moccassined feet, Wilf looked like he belonged in a fairy tale himself. Under a bridge, maybe. "How'd you like Snow White in her glass coffin?"

"Saran wrap coffin, you mean," said Ruby, leaning over the table with the last of the pudding in the pan. Under the light, her yellow hair sprang black and grey at the roots. "Who wants to clean this up?"

Harvey grinned up at her and she plopped the spongy chocolate mess onto his plate and went back to her stool. She leaned over to tip the coffee maker toward her cup, and was rewarded by a thin, dark dribble. She gave it a bleak look.

"Son of a bitch," said Ruby. "I really needed that cup of coffee."

Matthew got up and dumped the coffee grounds into the big garbage container, rinsed out the coffee maker and started to refill it. Ruby sniffled, and Matthew remembered, too late, that kindness always made her cry.

"Weren't the pelicans wonderful?" said Ruth, a sad-looking woman about Matthew's age. It was the first time she'd joined in a conversation since her arrival, a week ago.

"Well, I didn't see the parade but I sure's hell seen them birds," said Harvey, who had fingers or parts of fingers missing on both hands. His wild white hair stuck out in all directions. "I think them big mothers landed on the river." He licked a hand-rolled cigarette shut, striking a wooden match with his thumbnail. Verla winced, as she always did when he lit a match, and Harvey grinned at her through the smoke. "Anybody see them land?"

"I did," Matthew said. "They were feeding down by the dam." He wished he hadn't said it, he wasn't ready to share the pelicans yet. "It's probably just a feeding stop," he added. But he knew better. Something about the decisive way they'd landed and lined up for their dinner.

"The size of those birds is something else, eh?" Wilf beamed. "I bet those things were six feet across."

"More like nine." Neil, the schoolteacher, a thin, sandy man with glasses, spoke up. "The wingspan of the white pelican is nine feet."

Wilf whistled respectfully. "Nine feet. Holy Jesus."

The people who hadn't seen the pelicans or didn't care about them, drifted away from the table with their coffee, and chairs were scraping in the lounge, cards already slapping on the table. The tv came on, to an ad for Molson's Light. Somebody made a comment and everybody laughed.

Matthew looked at the blackboard by the kitchen door, that announced the revolving division of labour in the house. It was Matthew's and Verla's week for dishes, but Verla's name was rubbed out and Ruth's chalked in.

"I traded with Ruth. I'm going to see *The Twilight Zone*," Verla explained. "It's all cleared with Donald." Donald was the director of the house; he was seldom there after five unless there was trouble. Like last week when Harvey got drunk and fell off the third floor fire escape, trying to sneak in. Harvey ate grass, like a dog, when he was sick, and he'd been grazing on the front lawn when Donald got there. He'd been so remorseful, Donald had given him one more chance.

"*The Twilight Zone,* eh?" Wilf said. "I hope you got somebody to hold your hand, Sunshine."

"Wouldn't you like to know?" She tweaked Wilf's beard, smiling down at him, then ran up the stairs to her room on the third floor. The sound of Verla's quick footsteps on the narrow stairs always had a strange effect on Matthew, an urge to laugh and weep at the same time. He still found it difficult to believe that this lovely child could really be an alcoholic.

Matthew scraped plates while Ruth cleared and wiped the table. Ruby sat down with her cigarettes and notebook to plan next week's menus. The coffeemaker chugged quietly on the clean counter and the electric clock above the sink made soft little whirring sounds.

Matthew liked doing dishes. The window over the sink looked out on an apple tree that had dropped its pale blossoms on the grass — Rafe sat there now with his harmonica. With his hands immersed in hot, soapy water, he could shut out the smell of old dust in old carpets, the defeated lounge, the naked forty watt bulb in the upstairs hall. Ruth was quietly efficient, and her hair was soft and grey and didn't alarm him like Ruby's did.

Doing something like washing dishes made it easier for Matthew to talk, and he was a good listener. Ruth told him her drinking had started when her husband died, five years ago; that she wasn't going back to the little town she came from, afraid it would start all over again; that she was looking for a job. That frightened her. She had never had a job. Her two grown children didn't know what to make of any of it.

"You'll be all right," Matthew told her. "Some things just take time."

"What about you, Matthew? Do you have a family?"

"No," Matthew said. He always felt embarrassed and ashamed when someone asked him this.

He showed Ruth where things belonged, and felt sorry when he had to wring out the dishrag and hang it over the tap. Wilf would sweep and mop the floor. He wanted to ask Ruth if she'd like to go for a walk, but he didn't have the nerve.

Matthew worked as night watchman in a museum of prairie artifacts. As he made the rounds, flashing his light on the pampered relics, in the rooms that looked as though the occupant had just that moment stepped out, he walked through old rooms of his own, also kept polished and ready to occupy at a moment's notice: the wife he had lost — he still dreamed about her sometimes — and the home; the signpainting business he had drunk away, the gentle, rolling countryside he'd painted so often as background to chesty Hereford bulls, Arabian horses, family farms; his mother, who had loved him more than he deserved, and whose funeral he couldn't face without a couple of stiff ones before and a hundred more after. All gone.

And sometimes he remembered the relief of a drink hitting his stomach, remembered only the spreading, forgetting glow of it, and had to force himself then to think of the hospital room. He had now gone three months without a drink.

He always stopped at the dam on the way home from work. There, with the waking city muted by falling water, the morning sky flashing with gulls, and the big, silent pelicans drifting out to feed, something eased around Matthew's heart. As he smoked a cigarette and drank the last of the coffee in his thermos, the doors closed softly on those old rooms, and it was good. The best time of the day.

He worried about the pelican that didn't seem a part of the flock. It stayed out in the water while the others crowded together on the small island, opening and closing their long bills to the sky now and then, for all the world as if they were yawning. Matthew often stopped late at night on his way to work. He liked to see the island glowing whitely in the moonlight, liked knowing they were there. But even in the dark, he could often make out a single white shape apart from the rest.

August was stifling — the blistering heat pumped endlessly from some cosmic forge. The residents who slept on the steamy third floor of Hope Haven became morbid and snappish. Ruby cooked and wept and perspired. Even the narrow yard, where they gathered after supper on blankets and kitchen chairs, gave no relief till late at night, if then. As Matthew passed through the back yard on his way to work, the dim fire escape bloomed with light colored shirts and dresses, cigarettes moving like fireflies.

"Night, Matthew," they called. "Goodnight." As his tall figure passed by. "No rest for the wicked, eh, Matthew?"

Once, on his night off, he and Ruth went for a walk to the dam. When they came back, everyone but Rafe had gone out, and they sat together on the fire escape, the low, sweet notes of Rafe's harmonica drifting down from the third floor. They talked about the pelicans, the people at the house, Ruth's job hunt. They found a lot

of things to laugh about. Ruth was gradually losing the
sad, tired look she'd worn when she came to the house.
Matthew sat a couple of steps above her, and he found
it surprisingly easy to talk, his voice sounding deep and
pleasant, even to himself.

"You look very nice in that shirt, Matthew." She
smiled up at him. "The color suits you."

Matthew felt his face flush with pleasure. The shirt
was new, and he'd hoped she would like it. He shrugged.

"Gilding the lily," he said, and they both laughed.
"My mother used to say, 'Matthew isn't anything you'd
want to hang on a Christmas tree, but he's a good boy'."

Ruth smiled. A sudden breeze lifted her hair, brushing
it against her bare arm. It smelled like lilacs, Matthew's
favorite flower.

"You are, you know. Good. A good person."

"No," said Matthew, feeling suddenly uncomfortable.
And shortly after, he said he should turn in, though he
lay awake for hours.

August passed. Verla decided to go back to school,
and sat over books in the lounge, her brown feet bare
below her faded jeans. Neil got a teaching job in a small
town school and moved out. Ruth got a job in a drug-
store. Ruby got around to dyeing her hair. Rafe moved
a few steps closer to the others on the fire escape. A new
resident — a lawyer — had a terrible seizure in the
upstairs bathroom the night he moved in. Matthew saw
him looking at The Last Supper, inexpertly pushed out
in copper, which hung over the ugly imitation fireplace.
He looked puzzled. And slowly, slowly, by an infinit-
esimal amount, the empty space inside Matthew got
smaller.

One particularly sultry evening, Wilf and Matthew and Verla picked Ruth up from work and went for a drive. The back windows of Wilf's old car were painted over with brown paint. A relic of his drinking days, when he slept in the back seat.

"Enjoying the view back there?" Wilf laughed, as the car bounced and banged over a gravel road outside the city. Ruth sat beside Wilf, looking cool and fresh in her white uniform. Whenever they hit a hard bump, or made a left turn, Wilf's door flew open and he leaned way out to slam it shut. Ruth's hair fluttered. Dust settled in the folds of her uniform.

"Just like life, eh? This car?" Wilf shouted over his shoulder. "Ya can't look back. You gotta look ahead." He grinned at Verla in the rearview mirror. "Ain't that right, Sunshine?" The door flew open and he made a wild lunge for it. Verla was holding onto the front seat, giggling. She laughed a lot lately. "Yeah, Wilf. Whatever you say."

Ruth smiled over her shoulder at Matthew, and he realized, with a little shock of surprise, that he was having a good time. He was, in fact, having the time of his life, being shaken to pieces in Wilf's crazy old car. He even joined in when Verla started them singing.

"Feelin' good was good enough for meeeeee," Wilf sang lustily, his head thrown back, "Good enough for me an' Bobby McGee." Verla beat time on Matthew's bony knee.

When Wilf made a U turn and headed back they saw gigantic thunderclouds boiling up on the horizon. By the time they reached the city, the sky was black and the poplars along the boulevard were bent with the wind.

"Look at that sky," shouted Wilf. "Son of a gun, she's gonna pour."

"Look! Matthew, look!" Ruth pointed up over the castle-like Bessborough Hotel. The billowing slate sky was filled with soaring pelicans, their great white bodies tinged pink by the setting sun.

"Holy Jesus, look at that," Wilf said, as he swerved into a church parking lot near the Bessborough Park. As they ran across the street to the riverbank park, there was a sudden, ear-splitting crack of thunder. Verla screamed and Wilf laughed maniacally, grabbing her hand and pulling her along as the thunder rolled and rolled, like a timpani. In a grassy clearing, they stopped.

"Sweet Jumping Jesus," Wilf said softly.

Against the violent black sky, the big birds were riding the air currents. High above the glowing, golden-windowed castle, they criss-crossed in the air as if they'd rehearsed it, then half-closed their wings and dove wildly down the black sky to the rolling accompaniment of thunder. About forty feet from the ground, they pulled out of the dive and coasted back up again, their incredible white wings spread full out against the racing clouds. While the sky flashed and cracked, they rode it like a gigantic roller coaster, over and over again. Matthew looked back at the island, and saw one pelican bobbing on the green, whitecapped water.

Then, as the huge birds played their joyous game, the rain came at last, huge splats of it hitting their faces as they gazed up. Matthew felt a splash of water on his tongue, and realized that his mouth was open. As the rain came faster, Verla lifted her brown arms and twirled slowly around and around, her thin blouse soaking itself to her young breasts, as one by one the pelicans flew back downriver and made their awkward, kangaroo-hop landings on the island.

Wilf, who had actually been speechless while they watched the pelicans, now looked at Verla, beautiful in the rain, at Ruth and Matthew. His eyes were shining, and his beard streamed rivulets of rain.

"My God," he said. "I could have missed this. We all could have missed it."

And he didn't have to explain what he meant.

One morning as he came home from work, Matthew almost fell over Harvey, down on his hands and knees beside the back steps. He wasn't wearing a shirt or shoes.

"What are you doing?" asked Matthew, though he was afraid he knew. Harvey's greenish, perspiring face peered up at him.

"Sick," mumbled Harvey.

Matthew knelt beside him, patted him awkwardly on his damp, flaccid back. He smelled sour beer and vomit.

"Why did you do it? Now they won't let you stay at the house."

"I know." Harvey sat up, wiping his mouth with some grass. "Got a smoke, Matthew?"

He lit one and put it in Harvey's mouth. Harvey dragged on it, holding it between his thumb and third finger. All the rest were missing tips, or were missing altogether.

"Aw, what the hell," he said, finally. "I got nothin' to stay sober for."

Matthew sat down, folding his long legs inside his arms. They smoked in silence, watching a sparrow stalked by a tabby cat, silent as grey mist on the grass.

"I'm sixty-two years old," Harvey said, after awhile. "My old lady's left me. My kids don't talk to me. My drinkin' friends don't want nothin to do with me when

217

I'm off it.'' He dragged on the last of the cigarette, then put it beside Matthew's foot for him to step on. He stared at some point over Matthew's shoulder. ''The way I see it, there's sweet fuck-all to stay sober *for*.''

Matthew couldn't think of a thing to say. They were still sitting there when Donald came to work.

Matthew helped Harvey pack, and walked him to the bus stop.

''Don't take any wooden nickels,'' said Harvey, as he climbed on the bus.

Matthew looked across the river one morning and saw reds and golds blooming there, noted the encroaching ochre on the green island. The flock was restless, their habits changing. They swam back and forth, no longer piling together for long periods, and they spent more time in the air, in silent, perfectly synchronized flight. Matthew worried about the one. Hoped it would have sense enough to go when the time came.

He walked with Ruth through the streets of falling leaves, began to look forward to seeing her. He worried this new thing in his life as he walked the dim corridors of the museum, flashing his light into this or that dark corner. Those other rooms, the ones he had lived in for so long, had receded slightly, as if someone had drawn a gauze curtain there. Until the night he thought of Ruth, and knew, by the sudden thrust of joy in his chest, that he loved her.

Then out they came, his Furies, from the dark corners where they had merely been biding their time. *Ugly*, they hissed in his ear. *Failure*, they whispered. *Unlovable*, they sneered. Who do you think you are, they asked, that a good woman like Ruth would be interested in you?

He sat on the running board of a Model A Ford, and pressed his hands over his ears. It wasn't safe to love. He knew that. It was dangerous, dangerous, it left you with a big hole inside. He began to shake, like a man in shock. And suddenly Matthew wanted a drink more than he had ever wanted anything in his life. When the long night was finally over, he didn't go to the dam, and he didn't go to Hope Haven.

Matthew opened his eyes to a strange room, shut them against the glaring light. Pain splintered behind his eyes, sloshed in his head when he moved. The taste of bile burned rawly from throat to stomach, and his whole body, on top of the bedspread, felt fragile as a Christmas ornament.

With a hand over his eyes, he shakily reached up and fumbled for the switch on the bedside lamp, turning it off. It was dusk. What day he didn't know. Tuesday was the last day he remembered. Where he was he didn't know, either, not even what city. He had wakened in strange cities before, and sometimes been unable to recall — ever — how he had got there.

Very carefully, he raised himself to a sitting position and lowered his feet to the floor, but the motion was too much. The room wheeled, and vomit erupted like lava just as he reached the bathroom. He heaved again and again as he cleaned up the mess. Then he realized that at some time since it all began, he had pissed his pants. On the bedspread, the large stain was still damp. Matthew sat on the floor by the bed, overcome by weakness and shame.

About two inches of whisky stood in a bottle on the

table, and he shakily sipped it, gagging with the first few swallows, till the lurching things in his stomach were finally stilled. There were other, empty bottles. Carefully, then, as if he were walking on ground glass, he went to the window and looked out. The Bessborough and the river were there. There were fewer leaves — the trees across the river white and skeletal against the brown bank. He had not gone far.

Looking at the grey sky, his head pulsing with pain, he remembered something. He had wakened on the bed to the sound of geese — faint at first, like dogs barking in the distance, then closer and louder till their clangorous honking filled the night, filled the air in the room where he lay. And left him, as it receded in the distance, with the space inside larger, darker, colder than it had ever been before.

Had they gone, too? Those others? Had their beautiful black-bordered wings passed over in the night, passed powerfully, silently over the city as he lay insensible in his own piss? He must go to the river to see. He had to know, had to go to the river. He drained the bottle, felt strength and resolve flow in with the whisky.

As the cold wind hit his sweating body, he began to shake. He walked with his head down, the collar of his jacket turned up, walked with a sense of purpose, and it was still light when he arrived at the lookout.

It was empty, cold — dry leaves skittering across it. The island was deserted. Where the water spilled darkly over the dam, there was no huge, ugly bird waiting to scoop up yet another fish. Not one. He searched the grey, uncompromising sky in every direction, searched out every island. They were gone. All of them. Matthew took a deep, careful breath.

On the path to the river, sharp twigs jutted and snagged at his clothes. When he reached the place where the cement apron met the frothing water from the dam, he stopped. The river was fast and deep there. Matthew sat down to wait for dark. He remembered how he had felt before the ambulance came — the seductive sensation of peace that had stolen through him as more and more of his blood had pooled on the rooming house floor, and wondered, in an indifferent kind of way, if this would be like that.

He was wet with sweat, his jacket too light to keep out the cold, and he shook like a thin, dry pod, rattling in the wind. He smelled of urine. He wondered vaguely how many days since he had eaten, not that it mattered. He looked out at the empty island, the water, the sky. As clearly as if it had been burned into his brain, he saw the inexpressible beauty of the pelicans against the wild black sky. And he saw, as if he had been there, the silent dignity of their leaving, twenty-eight pairs of wings stroking as one.

And he thought of other things. Verla's wet brown arms as she danced in the rain, her hopeful steps on the stairs; Ruby, crying and banging pots in the big kitchen; Wilf and Rafe, and crazy, sad Harvey; Ruth. The shabby house that had, after all become a home. Staring across at the deserted brown island, Matthew waited.

Then Wilf was beside him, grabbing his arm, hanging on as if he knew he mustn't let go, even for a moment. Wilf, who must have come silently down the path and across the cement in his moccassins, though Matthew mightn't have heard him for the falling water.

"Hey, Matthew, hey man. I don't believe it! Holy

shit, am I glad to see you!'' His little eyes gleaming in
the dusk. ''We've been down here a hundred times, looking for you.'' He was holding on with both hands, pulling
at Matthew, pulling him painfully to his feet, Matthew
allowing it, too weak to get away, even from little Wilf.

Wilf pushed Matthew ahead of him, toward the path.

''God, I really don't believe this. We thought you were
in the river. Goddam it, why'd you hafta do that? What
happened you had to get drunk? Eh?''

Wilf pushed faster as the words came faster. Matthew
stumbled. ''Sorry.'' Helping him up. Pushing him on.

''You're crazy, you know, I got a good notion to kick
your skinny ass into the middle of next week.'' Pushing
with his hand on the small of Matthew's back. ''And
you don't smell like Chanel Number Five, either. Is that
what you want?''

''It's been godawful around the house . . . Ruby bawl-
ing her head off and cooking worse shit than ever . . .
Ruth looking for you everywhere, and shut up in her
room the resta the time.'' Somewhere, under the sickness
that threatened to collapse him right there on the path,
Matthew registered that. ''Verla, too. Missed an exam
out lookin' for you.''

''And you were just going to jump in the river, weren't
you? Well, if you ever take another drink you won't hafta
jump because I'll fucking well throw you in . . . You
hear?'' Matthew heard, but it took everything he had
to just keep putting one foot ahead of the other on the
steep slope.

Wilf stopped to sneeze, and Matthew stood swaying
like a tree.

''Five days of chasing around to bars and freezing my
ass off down here. I've got a cold and it's your fault.''
And so on it went, all the way up the path.

They were waiting by Wilf's old car, Ruth's white uniform the first thing Matthew saw when he came over the rise. The joy in her face. Verla's smile. "Everybody in the car!" Wilf shouted like a general. And they got in the back seat as Wilf got Matthew into the front, running around and leaping into the driver's seat as if Matthew might escape before he got there. Matthew hadn't the strength to turn the handle.

Wilf turned and grinned at the others. "Well, here he is. Here's Matthew." He smacked the steering wheel and yelled, "*Son of a bitch, we found him!*"

Matthew's head splintered. Over his shoulder, Verla's smile lit up the back of the car.

"Thank God," said Ruth, in her quiet voice.

For a moment, there was silence. Then Verla reached for him, hugging his ugly, whiskery face to her smooth cheek, and he felt her tears, wet on his face. "Oh, Matthew. We were so scared."

"Scared shitless," Wilf agreed, his grin threatening to split his face. "Have you had enough?" he asked, giving Matthew's shoulder a shake. Matthew thought he would pass out. Then Wilf scooted across the seat and put his arms around Matthew, too.

"I've never been in so fucking many bars in my whole fucking life," he said, starting to laugh. "Isn't that right?" he asked them, and they all laughed, agreeing with him. "Every grungy bar in town," said Verla, and they laughed some more. Ruth reaching for him, too. All of them touching, holding him in an awkward tangle. He was chilled through and they contained his shaking with their bodies, paid no attention to his silence.

Suddenly from deep inside Matthew, from the empty place where he had lived for so long, the sobs erupted, tearing at his throat with their violence, jolting his thin body over and over. No one said ''don't'', they just let him. And held him, and warmed him, and breathed on him.

''Oh, God,'' he said, finally, his voice sounding hoarse, unused. ''Oh, God.''

And he opened his arms and let them in.

NOTES ON AUTHORS

JOAN CLARK
b. 1934 Liverpool, Nova Scotia. Moved to Cape Breton, graduated from Acadia University, taught in Maritimes and Alberta. Married, 3 children, lives near Calgary. Has published 3 children's books and one book of short stories.

MERNA SUMMERS
Grew up on an Alberta farm, worked for 8 years as a reporter for the Edmonton Journal, and later did freelance journalism and radio work. Has published 2 books of short stories.

GERTRUDE STORY
b. 1929 on a Saskatchewan farm. Has worked as a freelance writer and broadcaster for over 20 years. 1984-85 first artist-in-residence in Prince Albert, Sask. Has published 2 books of short stories and 1 of poetry.

SHARON BUTALA
b. 1940 in a northern outpost, spent first 4 years in the bush. Graduated from University of Saskatchewan, worked as a special educator in Saskatchewan and Nova Scotia. Now married to a rancher and living in Eastend, Sask. Has published 1 novel.

BEVERLY HARRIS
b. in Montreal, educated at Sir George Williams University. Presently living in Calgary, teaching creative writing and co-editing Dandelion magazine.

GLORIA SAWAI
b. in Minneapolis, grew up in Saskatchewan and Alberta. Now lives in Camrose, Alta. with her 2 teenagers. Has had several plays produced.

BRENDA RICHES
b. in India, educated in England. Came to Saskatchewan in 1974, became editor of Grain magazine 1983. Has published 1 collection of stories and poems.

BONNIE BURNARD
b. 1945 in SW Ontario. Lived in northern Ontario and B.C. before moving to Saskatchewan in 1974. Became fiction editor of Grain 1983.

EDNA ALFORD
b. in Livelong, Saskatchewan. Has lived in Saskatchewan and Alberta, taught at Saskatchewan Summer School of the Arts. Has published 1 book of short stories.

CAROL SHIELDS
b. in Chicago. Has lived in Ottawa and now Winnipeg. Teaches at University of Manitoba. Mother of 5. Has published 2 books of poetry, 3 novels, 1 book of criticism.

DIANE SCHOEMPERLEN
(   ) in Canmore, Alta.

EUNICE SCARFE
b. in the U.S.A. Has lived and taught in England and Alberta. Married, 2 daughters. Presently in Japan.

CATERINA EDWARDS
b. 1948 in England. Came to Calgary in 1956. Teaches at University of Alberta and Grant MacEwan Community College. Mother of 2. Has published 1 novel.

SANDRA BIRDSELL
b. 1942 in rural Manitoba. Lives in Winnipeg, is president of the Manitoba Writers Guild. Has published 1 book of short stories.

LOIS SIMMIE
b. 1932 in Edam, Sask. Grew up in small, Saskatchewan towns, graduated from business college, worked, raised 4 children. Now lives in Saskatoon. Has published 2 books of short stories, 1 novel.